ABOUT MANY THINGS...
THOUGHTS TO STIR THE SOUL

W. Thomas Faucher

ISBN 0-9664787-1-1

All articles in this book were originally published in *The Bulletin*, Bend, Oregon, 1996-2001.The article titles used in this book may differ in some instances from *The Bulletin* titles.

Cover photograph of the Monastic Garden of Quarr Abbey, Isle of Wight. Photo used with permission. Illustration of St. Edward Church on page 33 by Charlotte K. Milam.

Published by
Kern O'Neil Publications
P.O. Box 104
Sisters, Oregon 97759

Printed in the United States of America
by Maverick Publications
Bend, Oregon

Dedication

I am honored to dedicate this book to four special mentors who entered the resurrection during the years it was written:

Eloise and Patrick Bieter
Reverend Blaise Turck O.S.B.
Right Reverend Monsignor Matthew Canon Kelly

Acknowledgments

All my writings come from the work and wisdom of many people. I want to acknowledge and thank a few of those who helped make my columns and this book possible:

The staff of the Diocesan Offices of the Diocese of Baker who have critiqued and improved all my columns;

The editors and staff of *The Bulletin* newspaper in Bend, Oregon, especially Gordon Black, John Costa, Carolyn Lamberson, Denise Costa, and Joy Rodgers;

The staff of Saint Edward the Martyr Parish, especially Carol Lippert and Mary Giraudo;

David and Marlene Simpson and Gary Asher.

I thank in a special way the wonderful people of Central Oregon of all (and no) religions, who have inspired me to write, and whose souls – I hope – my thoughts have stirred.

Introduction

"Water occupies a central place in traditional desert architecture, frequently in a cool courtyard. Father Faucher's writings are like finding such a deep well, filled with clear sweet water that quenches one's thirst."

John Kvapil, Architect

"I eagerly look forward to reading Father Faucher's insightful, stimulating columns. As a pastor I find them invaluable in helping my parishioners reflect on and discuss the real tough issues Christians face in today's world. They also shed much clarity on why we Presbyterians feel so much unity and connection with our Roman Catholic brothers and sisters. We need more people like Father Faucher with the gift of writing that opens our minds and our hearts. Courageous words from a courageous Christian leader!"

Rev. Patricia Campbell-Schmitt
Co-Pastor, First Presbyterian Church
Bend, Oregon

"Working in the hospice community as a chaplain, I have been in contact with people from all faith traditions. It is a joy to consistently hear that Father Faucher's work builds bridges of respect and introduces a public perspective in our community that is truly 'catholic' in the fullest sense of the word."

Richard Groves
Director
Sacred Art of Living Center
Bend, Oregon

"Father Faucher's clear style and his ability to deal with religious subjects frequently stimulates much thought whether the reader agrees with him or not. He reaches out to all, no matter what their religious persuasion or lack of it. He always accomplishes this without being offensive or combative. His sensitive and comprehensive understanding to the teachings of the Catholic Church influences all his articles. He is an articulate voice helping others to understand the 'Catholic point of view' without being overly dogmatic or arrogant. I feel that Father Faucher's articles are a blessing that continues to enlighten and inspire those who read them."

Father Martin Haggins O.F.M. Cap.
Pastor, St. Francis of Assisi Catholic Church
Bend, Oregon

'One time Father Faucher said to me, "You just gave me inspiration for an article when you said 'Once upon a time we used to call it original sin, now we call it dysfunctional families.'" Father Faucher is a born writer and original thinker. His mind is going all the time and he has the ability to collect trivia and see the inscape, to make the connections for us mere mortals and bring us to another level of understanding. Sensitive....comprehensive....challenging. He has been able to present the truth in an historical setting that is acceptable to his readers. His articles have been a great asset in bridging the gap between different creeds and traditions while not riding roughshod over others beliefs, rather with a sensitivity and deftness that defies contradiction.'

Father Brian McKenna O.F.M. Cap.
Associate Pastor
St. Francis of Assisi Catholic Church
Bend, Oregon

'Father Faucher's contribution to the civilizing of religious discussion has been nothing short of magnificent. I come to this as the grandson of an Orangeman and a skeptic of religion. His contribution through his monthly columns to the necessity for religious polity and his teaching of the history of religion have been heartening to me and, I believe, a great contribution to the prevention of bigotry in Central Oregon. As John Donne might have said, no place, including central Oregon....."is an island unto itself." So Father Tom will go down in the history of this region as a genuine contributor to a more civil and generous society. I would travel miles just to listen to his sermons and enjoy his friendship.'

Bruce Bishop
President
High Desert Forum
Bend, Oregon

"They say that the Holy Spirit works in mysterious ways. I can only affirm that the effect of Father Faucher's writings and the convergence of other events in my life have profoundly altered me. These articles started a process that has given me new lenses to not only view life, but to engage in life. His articles have challenged readers to not only look at themselves and their beliefs, but to also understand the history and context of our institutions and our relationship within them. He is not afraid to admit error or challenge orthodox (rigid) thinking. Faith and reason are not an oxymoron; with greater knowledge and reflection can come faith. The question is then not 'why,' but 'why not?' His own humanity and search come through in his writings. With his assistance, I have seen our greater connectedness and community. Needless to say, I would not be where I am today had it not been for Father Faucher's articles."

John Gregory
Parishioner
St. Edward the Martyr Catholic Church
Sisters, Oregon

"I have been reading Father Faucher's monthly columns ever since they began to be published. I have found them to be very interesting, enlightening, and stimulating. He manages to speak of religion and faith in a fresh and original way. Although, such church doctrines can be very abstract, he seems to be able to find concrete and practical examples so people can relate what he writes to their every day lives. Moreover, he almost invariably makes me think by the way he approaches each topic. I have also noticed that his columns are of interest to people of many different faiths. He writes in such a way that people of different faiths always seem to be able to understand what he is talking about. I know I will refer to this collection of his columns many times in the future."

Father Mike Walsh O.F.M. Cap.
Associate Pastor
St. Francis of Assisi Catholic Church
Bend, Oregon

"I read Father Faucher's columns as a former Catholic whose husband and teenage daughter recently converted to Catholicism. I also read the columns in search of material to mail to my two young sons and their wives; the wives are Catholic, the sons are not. If the soul is the essence of the individual, then Father's columns embody the soul of what I have sought to nurture within our family. They often address ways to approach the world and its inhabitants: lovingly, respectfully, without being judgmental. Their value is in their relevance to the every day as well as to the spiritual. In fact, they remind us that true spirituality is in the every day, not something to be considered only on Sunday. Just as the concept 'to stir' has several definitions, Father Faucher's words remind us that the soul can be stirred in many ways. The varied stew that is simmering in our family pot has been greatly enhanced by the spice of his columns."

Margie Gregory
Social Worker
Bend, Oregon

"Father Faucher provides for his readers real insights into the meaning of human spirituality—not only for individuals, but for organizations and institutions. He addresses the human condition and its struggles from a different perspective of both religion and spirituality and allows us to understand the difference. His columns have raised many contemporary issues for contemplation and discussion which certainly add tremendous value to those of us who are interested in both the spiritual health of the individual and our organizations."

James T. Lussier
President
St. Charles Medical Center
Bend, Oregon

"If you want to be challenged in your moral and spiritual beliefs....read this book! These stimulating articles cover subject matter that few of the clergy have the courage to broach publicly. Only a person who is confident in his own beliefs could undertake to present views to which he it totally opposed, in such an honest manner. And only someone like Father Faucher could then refute those views with civility."

Mervin Kerzner
Member of the Jewish Community
Bend, Oregon

Contents

October 24, 1996

Religion Puts Life, World In Context

I get together fairly often with people I grew up with. Since I am a priest the subject of religion comes up once in awhile, including the topic of why some of us have religious faith and some do not.

There are more people who do not go to church in Oregon and Washington than in almost any other states. Sociologists and phenomenologists of religion tell us the reasons for this are complicated, but boil down to both a sense of freedom and independence and a lack of strong roots or ethnic ties.

Why have some of my friends chosen to have religious faith and to be active in churches, while others claim some faith in God but don't want anything to do with church, and still others just say that God and religion have no meaning to them at all? There is some correlation between those who grew up in religious households and those who go to church now, but not much. For most of us our view of God and religion is very much a personal adult decision.

As a individual who has chosen to spend my life as a religious person and to make religion my life's work as a member of the clergy, friends who see no value or worth in religion challenge me, they make me think, they force me to reflect on why I have made the choices I have made. At the same time my life decisions challenge them. I cause them to think.

I would like to share with you some of my observations about why I am religiously active.

We all tend to do what it is our own self-interest, what we feel is good for us. My belief in God, my faith in the church, my religious practice is good for me, it tells me who I am. By having a relationship with God I am able to see where I fit into the world, into the universe. I am able to answer the questions of why there is life, what am I doing here, what is it all about.

I am a person who learns from experience. I have had a lot of experiences in life. In seeking to understand those experiences I

1

find that faith in God enables me to make sense of them, to see what is true within them and recognize what is false. My faith in God is my personal spirituality.

I see myself as created by a God who knows, enjoys, likes, and loves me. When I establish a relationship of thankfulness and gratitude with God I come to know, enjoy, like, and love God as well.

But having just a personal one-on-one relationship with God is not enough for me, I need to share that relationship with others and have them share their relationships with God with me. I want and need to live out my spirituality, to put into practice what I say I believe.

Religion enables me to do that. When I check my experiences and my faith with the faith of my religion I find support and confirmation of my experiences and my conclusions. Everything that has happened to me is comprehensible when seen through the eyes of my religious faith.   I need and want the support, encouragement, strength, and enjoyment that comes from shared love, and that is for me the practice of religion. My sacramental life in the church gives me strength when I am weak, down, depressed, sinful, lonely. But it also gives me ways to rejoice and celebrate when I am strong, well, and happy.

I know who God is, who I am, and who all those around me are because of my faith and the living out of that faith in religion. That is why I have made the choices I have made.

Give Thanks And Celebrate Humanity

A good case can be made that the highest human characteristic, that which distinguishes us most from all other creatures is not intelligence, for other animals have that. Nor is it affection or even love, for again we can find many examples of those attributes in the animal kingdom. No, what most sets humans apart from all other creatures is the ability to give thanks.

Giving thanks is the most awesome thing a human being can do. It is the core of love; it is the apex of a relationship. It requires great intelligence to give thanks, as well as true faith, real hope, authentic maturity, and functional humility.

Giving thanks takes a great deal of work. First of all you have to be able and willing to experience receiving something from someone else. Then you have to be aware, actually understand, that experience. Next you have to make a judgement about that experience. Finally you have to decide to do something about it — give thanks.

These four steps — "experience", "understanding", "judgement", "decision" — form the basis for all truly human actions, and they are most fully expressed in the act of thanksgiving.

The basis for true Christianity, true Christian spirituality, is giving thanks. It is not standing before God like some beaten dog, mistake of creation, or even guilty sinner. Our primary relationship with God is that of giving thanks for all the many and splendid gifts we have received, beginning with life itself and going on to all the relationships of love that surround us.

Christianity is based on honesty and truth. The honest truth is that God created us to so that he could enjoy loving us, and so that we could love him in return. Our relationship with God is one of noble lovers, expressed by Jesus when he told us to call the Father, "Abba", that is "Daddy".

Thus the first and most important Christian prayer is "Thank You". All conversations with God, from asking for forgiveness to seeking help, flow from that original act of thanking God for everything.

All our relationships with other people imitate our relationship with God, and thus all healthy human relationships are also based on giving thanks. Authentic honest thanksgiving includes responsibility, praise, repentance, enjoyment, satisfaction, and all the other attributes of a healthy relationship.

I have met people who would not give thanks to anyone. There was the sullen kid in jail who said he had not one to thank because no one had ever done anything for him. There was the wealthy young business tycoon who viewed himself as a self-made man. He owed his success to no one but himself. There was the old woman whose marriages had all ended in divorce. What these "thankless" people have in common is bitter, humorless, grumpy, vile dispositions.

These people also share the belief that giving thanks demeans them, makes them less than someone else, and makes them vulnerable. They are wrong in thinking thanksgiving demeans the person giving thanks, but correct in thinking that it makes that person vulnerable.

Acknowledging vulnerability is part of any healthy relationship, whether it be with God or with another human being.

True Christianity is based on giving thanks to God, on being honest with yourself and with God, on being thankful and in love with those around us. True Christian worship is the expression of this thankfulness, the living out of a relationship of thanks between God and the individual and the community.

Good religion is good mental health. Giving thanks is human healthfulness at its best.

December 27, 1996

A Christmas Letter To A Friend

Dear Daniel,

So for Christmas you want to see God.

That's a awesome desire, but not an easy request. God is almost never seen face to face. Only a few very special people, like Moses or maybe Francis of Assisi have actually looked upon the face of God. The rest of us can feel God, hear God, taste God, smell God, and touch God, but we can only see him in his reflection. We know where he is through the marvelous signs of his presence.

Like ripples on water, God is known by what happens when he is there. When God is present, people who are blind begin to see. When God's around, lame people walk. When God is in the room, hungry people are fed. When people who are thirsty are given drink, God is right there doing it. When the poor have good news given to them, God is there.

God told us that where there is knowledge and love, he is there. When human beings get an education and learn the truths of life, the truths of faith, the truths of hope and charity, God is there. When people are loved, cherished, revered, given their dignity, treated with honor, allowed to be free, then God is present in each of those actions.

God is at home when people are patient and kind. God is there when they are not jealous, not rude, not self-seeking, when people do not put on airs, are not prone to anger.

All sorts of things happen where God lives, prisoners find freedom, captives find liberty, sinners find forgiveness, strangers are welcomed, orphans and widows are cared for, and the poor are given hope and love.

The joy of God presence is not just a feeling, it is an odor. It is a smell the permeates everything, and it is joined by the fragrances of kindness, peace, patience, benignity, wisdom, and hospitality. Together they create a bouquet of virtues that changes everything and everyone.

Touching God is like the lion lying down with the calf, the child putting his hand in the cobra's lair, and the wolf being the guest of the lamb. We touch God when we judge not by appearance nor by hearsay, when we measure out with honesty, when we fill in the valleys and make the rough places smooth.

The presence of God fills our ears when we hear the music of creation, the symphony of the birds, the concerto of the waterfalls, the aria of a newborn child, the silence of an isolated desert, the opera of daily life, the words of forgiveness.

The absence of God is as apparent as his presence. When we murder, steal, cheat, lie, and cause pain, then there is no room for God. God's absence is horrible, and we can feel it, see it, smell it, hear it, and touch it. If we do touch the absence of God our hands sting with a pain that can only be graced away.

Daniel, my friend, you have already touched, heard, smelled, and tasted God. You have seen him in the people who surround you and love you. You experimented with his absence and found yourself on the road to self-destruction. But you felt God's hand, heard his voice, tasted his love, and you came to life once more.

And just as you once saw, felt, heard, and touched God in the people who loved you, so now you are the source of God for others. You fulfill your Christmas wish, you see the face of God, when you see the faces of the people of the world who love one another, and that includes your face as well. For our faces are a true and accurate reflection of the face of God.

Merry Christmas, Peace and Love,

Tom

January 30, 1997

It's True – Money Can't Buy Happiness

I grew up with a man [let's call him Stan] who is now very wealthy — like hundreds of millions of dollars wealthy. I see him every once in awhile and we are still friends. Stan is probably one of the most unhappy people I know.

He is so unhappy it is almost a subject of humor when I do see him. He feels it is unfair that he has made all of this money, he has dreamed the American dream, he has done everything that should be done, while I have not. Yet I am happy and he is not.

One of the reasons that he and I are still friends is that I told him I would never ask for or accept money from him. The last time we met it was at a coffee shop and I bought the coffee.

Stan has had three wives and is presently divorced. He has two grown children he rarely sees. His daughter lives with a rock musician in Italy and his son owns a youth hostel at a ski resort. Both kids have been in treatment for drug use.

Stan grew up in some church but doesn't go anymore. He finds Christianity in any of its forms too restricting, and thinks that ministers and priests ask for too much money from people. [When I reminded him that the garage at one of his homes cost more than the church building where I am pastor he just shrugged.]

Stan's questions to me were, "Why am I unhappy? Is God punishing me and making me unhappy? Does God hate rich people?"

My answer to Stan was simple — he has made choices and he is enjoying the consequences of his choices. He has done nothing to make himself happy so he is not happy. God doesn't have anything to do with it. Happiness is not connected to being rich or poor. Happiness is a result of decisions we make.

Every time there was a choice between pleasure and joy, Stan chose pleasure. From his high school affair with the student teacher, to his affair with a client while married to his first wife, to all his subsequent sexual adventures, his life has been all for his own temporary pleasure. He loved work and disliked children so he neglected his own kids. He climbed the success ladder over the bodies of betrayed comrades and now has few friends left. He enjoyed watching rivals fall, their careers destroyed.

After a lifetime of such pleasurable activity he has the gall to try to blame God for his problems — Stan's problems are all of his own making. What God did was make a world in which we are responsible for the consequences of our own decisions. Goodness is its own reward and sin is its own punishment.

Stan thought money, sex, and power would bring him pleasure — and they have. But pleasure is not the same as joy or happiness. Pleasure fades quickly, and when pleasure is not connected to goodness and joy it has a bitter aftertaste. He is choking now on the residues of the very pleasures that made him who he is.

Why Stan still sees me I don't really know. Maybe it is because I never tell him what he wants to hear, as do all the people he has working for him. Maybe it is that I tell him it is never too late to change and become a good person. Or perhaps it is just nostalgia for a happier time many years ago when we were both young and just beginning.

Stan told me when I last saw him that "if" I'm right and God lets us live with the consequences of our own choices, then God shouldn't have given us those choices. He is determined to find a way to blame someone else for his unhappiness rather than himself, but he will not succeed in doing so. Stan is a self-made man.

February 28, 1997

It Is Not The Purpose Of Church To Cure

A child was sent to the store on an errand. She did not return when expected and her father, going out to hunt for her, found her finally headed for home. The girl explained that she had been delayed because she had come across her friend, who had dropped her favorite china doll on the sidewalk.

"It was all broken," she solemnly told her father.

"I'm sorry," he responded. "It was nice of you to stay and help her pick up the pieces."

"Oh, no," she said. I stayed to help her cry."

It is very easy to make a serious mistake when we think about church, about religion. The mistake is to think that church is to *cure* our brokenness, sinfulness, weakness. Church does not cure, church helps us *care* for our brokenness, sinfulness, weakness.

It is easy to make that mistake because we want instant magic cures for what is wrong with us. We don't like the parts of us which are broken, especially if we did the breaking. We know that sin is self-destructive behavior, and that we cause our own pain. But we want someone else to take it away.

Even if we are not the source of the wound, when we have been sinned against and the pain, the hurt has been caused by another we want to be cured. We want the pain to go away, we want relief. That is what society promises us — every pain can be taken away if you just take the right pill, drink the right medicine, do the right exercises.

In this view, if church is going to have a place in this society, it had better deliver the goods, it had better be able to cure spiritual wounds. If church doesn't make us feel better then it has no value, for value is based on what it can do for us.

This is the way many of us are tempted to think, to view church and religion as another optional means of instant relief and gratification, this one specifically designed for the soul. God is supposed to

9

be some divine grandma who kisses us when we harm ourselves and makes it all better. In this view church becomes magical incantations and colorful rituals that instantly put the pieces of the china doll back together again.

People who think this way say they have tried church — "been there, done that" — and found that it just doesn't work for them. The usual complaint is that they get nothing out of it.

People who want instant relief and gratification from religion are never going to get anything out of it, because that is not what church is. They are people playing golf with bowling balls and complaining that the ball doesn't fit in the hole.

The worship of God that is church is not a magic cure. Worship is an act of giving thanks which we and God do together that cares for us. We bring our wounds, created by us or by someone else. These can be healed, which is far different from being cured, but the healing takes a long, long time, and comes from being cared for. And even when there is healing the scars — the consequences — remain.

We are cared for by God directly and by God through our fellow broken and scarred brothers and sisters, and we care for them. The care comes in the countless ways we come to truly understand and believe that no matter what we look like, what we have done, how broken and wounded we may be, we are still known, loved, and wanted, both by God and by our brothers and sisters.

Church is God and the people who help us laugh, and when we need to, help us cry.

March 21, 1997

A Guide To Holy Week

What a storyline — adulation, praise, betrayal, food, drink, politics, blood, humanity, divinity, pain, humiliation, religion, deceit, torture, death, resurrection! Holy Week has it all.

For most Christians it is the most important time of the year. In the liturgical and traditional churches [those which pray with gestures and ceremonies as well as words] each of the days of Holy Week has its own special history and form of celebration. Much of the tradition comes from legends, myths, stories that have grown and accumulated over the years. Some of it is biblical in origin some is not. But the essential elements of each day are founded in the scriptural accounts of the last days of Jesus.

PALM SUNDAY

Also called Fig Sunday or Passion Sunday. On Palm Sunday the Christian people celebrate the triumphant entry of Jesus into Jerusalem. In the liturgical churches people are given blessed palm branches and there is often a procession outside the church building. The Gospel reading for Palm Sunday is one of the Passion Narratives read or sung by three lectors with all the people having a part. After Mass or the service people take the palm branches and hang them on the walls of the home, often after braiding them into crosses, towers, or crowns.

MONDAY AND TUESDAY OF HOLY WEEK

On these days the liturgical churches follow the Gospel stories of Jesus during the first Holy Week. He was staying the night either at Gethsemani or in Bethany [both near Jerusalem], and would come into the city and spend the day preaching at the Temple.

Events that took place on the days just before or just after Palm Sunday include a banquet in Bethany where a woman anoints his feet with oil and Judas Iscariot objects; the cursing of a fig tree which does not have fruit; and condemnation of Jerusalem; and the expulsion of the moneychangers from the temple. The anger of the religous authorities at Jesus increases.

SPY WEDNESDAY

This is the day remembered for the actions of Judas Iscariot who goes to the chief priests and agrees to betray Jesus. They needed someone to tell them where he would be at night so that he could be arrested quietly without a big crowd all around him.

In addition to the regular Masses and sections of the Divine Office normal to every day, this day had a special celebration that has almost disappeared. Late in the evening in some cathedrals a service called "Tenebrae" was celebrated.

It was a public singing of matins and lauds [two parts of the old Divine Office] in a spirit of mourning. A triangular candlestand of 15 candles was slowly extinguished one by one as the psalms and prayers were said. At the end a prayer was offered in the darkness and all withdrew.

HOLY THURSDAY

Also called Maundy Thursday or Shear Thursday. In the liturgical churches this day begins the "Triduum", the Three Great Days. Once the Evening Mass of the Lord's Supper begins it is one continuous service until the end of the First Mass of Easter on Saturday night. No other sacraments or services [weddings, funerals, baptisms, or even confessions except in emergencies can be celebrated] from this time on.

At the Lord's Mass or Service the feet of people are washed [usually twelve people]. At the end of Mass the Blessed Sacrament or Reserved Eucharist to be used on Good Friday is carried to a special chapel with flowers representing the garden, the procession winding throughout the church in memory of Jesus leaving the Upper Room and going to Gethsemani. Just as Jesus and apostles spent time there in prayer, so are people asked to do so today. The church itself is stripped of everything movable.

Many families eat lamb at home on Holy Thursday in honor of the Passover Meal.

GOOD FRIDAY

The official liturgy of Good Friday is the oldest ritual in christianity, changed very little since the early centuries. The Eucharist [Mass] cannot be celebrated, giving rise to the Anglican name of the "Service of the Pre-Sanctified" meaning that Holy Communion comes from hosts consecrated the night before.

For the liturgy the people assemble in the barren church and the priest and ministers enter in total silence. A prayer is said, the lessons are read, and the Passion is proclaimed by three readers and the people. After the homily the ancient General Intercessions are sung, followed by the unveiling of the cross and its veneration. The distribution of Holy Communion consecrated the night before completes the service and all leave in silence.

Many private devotions are also held on Good Friday such as Stations of the Cross or a prayer service called the "Tre Ore" [traditionally the three hours Jesus was on the cross, from noon until 3 PM].

HOLY SATURDAY

Technically this day does not exist in Christian liturgical tradition. No service, no sacrament, nothing can be done on this day until the beginning of Easter after sundown and the lighting of the Easter Fire.

What used to happen on Saturday was the completion of the Lenten fast at noon so cooking for Easter could begin, and traditionally churches are filled with people getting the buildings ready for the Easter Vigil and First Mass of Easter.

EASTER VIGIL AND FIRST MASS OF EASTER

The service of the Easter Vigil, which must begin between sundown and sunrise, is the most important event of the liturgical churches' year. Most churches start about 9 or 10 PM. As the people gather outside a fire is lit, symbolizing the act of resurrection and the restoration of light into a world plunged into darkness by the death of Jesus. A large ornate Paschal Candle is carved with symbols, blessed, and then lit. Small candles reminiscent of baptismal candles are lit by everyone from the Paschal Candle and carried into the church which is decorated but kept dark.

An ancient poem called the Exsultet is sung, and everyone is invited to go back in time and listen to the story of God's saving love for humankind by listening to nine Old Testament readings [often in

America these are reduced to just three readings].

In response to the readings the people sing the "Gloria", the lights are turned on, and the story of the resurrection is proclaimed in a reading from the Epistle and then the Gospel. The great Easter cry of "Alleluia" is sung for the first time since Ash Wednesday.

Following the homily are the rituals of baptism, consisting of the calling of those to be baptised, the Litany of the Saints, the Blessing of the Water, the Baptism [preferably by full immersion], then the celebration of Confirmation, and the reaffirmation of baptismal promises by everyone present. Mass then continues for the first time since Holy Thursday.

Other Easter traditions still used are the blessing and distribution of eggs as the symbol of resurrection, and the belief that those who eat an egg as their first food after the Easter Eucharist will always have Christ in their hearts.

EASTER SUNDAY

For the liturgical churches the celebrations on Sunday proper are a continuation of the great feast of the Easter Vigil with the singing of the Great Alleluia and the renewal of baptismal promises. It is fulfillment of a week of great grace, emotion, and growth.

In all churches visitors are always welcome to come and share in these great events, and thank God for the great gift of the life, death, and resurrection of His Son Jesus the Christ.

March 28, 1997

Did Jesus Really Rise From The Dead?

"If there had been a television camera focused on the tomb of Jesus that first Easter in Jerusalem two thousand years ago, what would it have seen?"

It's a valid and fair question. The central focus of the Christian faith in all its many forms is the death and resurrection of Jesus Christ. Even St. Paul said that if Jesus did not rise from the dead then our faith is in vain.

Most Christian churches share a common belief: Jesus was the second person of the Blessed Trinity who became a full human being. He was true God and true man. He physically died on the cross, was buried, and physically rose from the dead.

Various Christian churches differ on what each emphasizes in this truth; some stress the divinity or humanity of Jesus, some concentrate on his death, others focus on his resurrection. But all main Christian groups believe that God became man, died, and rose again.

But why do Christians believe Jesus rose from the dead? What proof is there? What would that television camera have seen that day at the base of the hill just outside the walls of Jerusalem?

For people with faith, physical proof of the resurrection is secondary to their experience of the Risen Christ. But both tradition and scripture testify that Jesus did rise.

The first testimony of the physical resurrection is the accounts found in the New Testament. All four Gospels tell a similar story, that it was women who first discovered the resurrection, and the men, including the apostles, did not believe them. No one of that day who wanted believers would have put women in such a prominent role as witnesses unless that is the way it really happened.

From the earliest days there have always been attempts to disprove the resurrection. These include the ideas that rather than die on the cross Jesus just slipped into a coma and after burial was revived; or that the apostles stole the body; or that no physical resurrection took place but a spiritual one; or that Jesus only had a temporary human form but was not really human. These and many other theories have been bantered around for many hundreds of years. The modern "Jesus Seminar" group has brought some of these theories back into discussion.

The Gospels themselves mention people who did not believe that Jesus had risen and tried to spread the story that the followers of Jesus had stolen the body. The Gospels also describe the resurrected body of Jesus as his real body.

One of the most important arguments for the physical resurrection of Jesus is the fact that the body was never found. For both the Jewish and Roman authorities displaying the body of Jesus would have stopped this new and dangerous Christianity in its tracks. There is no record in scripture or in Roman or Jewish literature that anyone ever claimed that the body had been found.

The followers of Jesus spent their lives spreading the word that Jesus had risen from the dead, and most of them died martyrs' deaths because they would not give up this belief. If they had stolen the body and then lied they would not have given their lives for something they knew to be untrue.

From the beginning Christian tradition has been totally consistent in the belief in the physical resurrection of Jesus. All the theories mentioned before and others have never been able to dislodge the sure conviction that Jesus died on the cross and rose from the tomb.

I firmly believe that Jesus did die and rise, I believe it because of my faith experiences of the Risen Christ and because every attempt to disprove it has failed.

"Turn on the television camera" — slowly the great stone begins to move — "zoom in for a close-up" — the edge of the opening appears — the stone is now rolling away — "move back for full shot" — a light can be seen inside the tomb — there is the faint outline of a body — "slowly move in" — now a face and hands can be seen — "get the body, close-up of the whole body" — it is Jesus, Jesus of Nazareth, Jesus the Christ — "now the face, close-up of the face" — it is the face of man, it is the face of God, risen from the dead.

April 18, 1997

Catching Faith Begins At Home With Parents, Kids Talking

A tenth grade student — let's call him John — in one of the area's schools told his parents that he was smoking pot and that he was sexually active. The impetus for this revelation was a discussion between John, his brother and sister, and their parents inspired by the call of a TV network for a family talk on drugs.

The family discussion was very difficult for all five family members, because they are a family who do not discuss, who do not share easily. Both parents came from families that did not show much physical affection. They resolved that they would show plenty of physical affection to their children and they have done this well. But there has been almost no intimacy between parents and children of feelings, values, hopes, and prayers.

John's parents are typical of many parents, both those active in religion and those who are not. They personally involve themselves to be good parents in many areas of life. But when it comes to religion and church they do not share intimately their deepest feelings and prayers.

That reality is changing. What it means to be a Christian parent is not what it once was. Christian parents of all kinds are being called upon to be the first and best of teachers in the faith of Jesus Christ. The hundreds of years of expecting someone else — priests, ministers, sisters, pastors, brothers, preachers, or the lady down the street — to teach faith to children has come to an end.

That era has come to an end because it does not work. Faith is not taught, it is caught. Faith comes from understanding and reflecting on the experience of knowing Jesus, feeling Jesus, absorbing Jesus. Theology and doctrine come from putting that experience-based faith into words. Catechism, bible classes, or other educational efforts come far down the path of sharing faith.

17

That path begins when parents intimately share their experience of Jesus with their children. When a father sits down with his children and tells them how he has come to know and love Jesus Christ, when he shares with them how he prays, when he exposes the times when being close to Jesus has been difficult — these are the times when faith is caught.

When a mother does not just teach her children how to form prayers, but truly shares how to open one's soul to God and how to listen to God, or when a mother can express what the true self-worth feels like — that is the experience of Jesus that brings faith.

But all too often parents themselves, even those who go to church, have never thought in those kinds of concepts, have never shared with themselves personally or with each other as a couple, the intimate details of their relationships with God.

Oregon is one of the states where most people say they believe in God but do not go to any church. Those parents also have the obligation to express and share with their children why they believe and live as they do.

During the coming month, I invite each family, church going and non-church going, to set up a specific special time when the following questions [worded to be asked by children, especially teenaged children] are answered by each parent, and then have a discussion. They are not easy questions, and parents may need some time to think about the answers first.

1. Mom, Dad, what is your relationship with God, and how has it gotten to be what it is?

2. Dad, Mom, what is God like, what does God think of you, what does God think of me?

3. Mom, Dad, what is the purpose of life, why am I here, what am I supposed to do with my life?

4. Dad, Mom, who is Jesus Christ and what does he mean to you, what should he mean to me?

5. Mom, Dad, how, when, why do you pray, and what does it do for and to you?

18

May 30, 1997

Toughest Debates Must Be Done With Dignity

I was visiting a rural county jail when the sheriff asked me if I wanted to sit in on a "discussion" with a man just arrested. The family had recently moved from the rural south and the thirteen year old daughter had said something at school indicating sexual activity with her father.

The man did not deny it, but seemed confused by the fuss. "What's the purpose of having daughters?" was his question. Society disagreed with him and imposed upon him the view that incest is morally and legally wrong.

Society imposes moral positions upon people all the time, including the view that possession of certain substances is wrong, or publication of certain materials is wrong.

Society's standards change. One example of this is that discrimination by race or gender — once enshrined into law — is now forbidden. Those who favor such discrimination find that a law has been imposed upon them.

What brings all of this to mind are discussions throughout Oregon, and nationally on such topics as Planned Parenthood, partial birth abortion, assisted suicide, and gay rights. Some people complain that in all of these issues other people's views are being imposed upon them. When one party to the discussion is a religion, then some of those on the other side complain about churches "legislating morality" or "imposing morality".

All civil laws are imposed morality. Somebody with enough clout gets the lawmaker to agree with him or her and a law is made imposing some action or prohibiting some action. In a democracy there is supposed to be discussion before the law is made or revised.

The opinions people bring to the discussion express their moral standards. Those standards may be broad or narrow, wide or specific, allowing many actions or favoring only a few. But all are moral standards. To advocate total sexual activity at all ages between both sexes is a moral position, just as is the advocacy of advocating sexual activity only between married adults, as are all other positions on the subject.

Religions, including Judaism, Islam, Christianity and others, have moral positions on subjects which affect human activity. These positions are based on that religion's understanding of the relationships between God and humanity and between human beings themselves.

These religious moral positions usually include two major responsibilities not shared by some individual moral positions: the responsibility to protect the members of society who have the least power, and the responsibility to promote the greatest good for all.

These responsibilities make religions a moral compass for a democratic society. Examples of this in American history include church activity in the moral debate on slavery before the civil war and churches activity in the civil rights struggle in the 1960s.

When churches fail to exercise this role society is harmed, as shown in the churches' silence when Japanese citizens were interred in World War II, or Indian land was stolen in the old west.

The coming months will force our area and society to debate moral issues. Society is best served when this debate centers on the issues and the facts involved. To this end some rules of debate may be in order.

1. All moral positions and opinions are free to be expressed and free to be debated. Each moral position and opinion must be evaluated and judged on the strengths of the foundation on which it rests. "What is the foundation for your opinion?" is always an appropriate question.

2. No moral position or opinion should be accepted or rejected on the personality of its presenter.

3. The media has the absolute obligation to report accurately and fairly, and check the accuracy of all anecdotes and alleged facts.

4. Religious teachings are fully acceptable as part of any discussion. Such teachings are subject to the same scrutiny and evaluation as all other positions.

5. Moral positions and opinions based solely on emotion, authority, fantasy, or desire are subject to rejection.

6. The greater good of all and the protection of the less powerful members of society are legitimate interests to be included in all aspects of all debates.

7. Political compromise may be possible, moral compromise may not be possible or even desirable.

8. Lies, misrepresentations, forged facts and all other forms of manipulation lose the perpetrator the right to continue in the debate.

9. The most popular moral position at any given time may not be the one that best serves society. Success at legislating a moral position does not automatically make that position the one that best serves society.

10. Personal attacks, religious attacks, or attacks upon religious beliefs are always unacceptable.

The coming months and years will seriously test the ability of our society to legislate what is truly best. If we do not choose to discuss and debate with dignity and a dedication to truth the laws we pass or do not pass will harm us for years to come.

June 27, 1997

Glee Over McVeigh's Death Troubling

The image was clear and powerful — a middle aged woman in a yellow dress coming out of the Federal Courthouse in Denver, her face wide in a smile of unrestrained glee. "Death!" she shouts to the waiting crowd and the television cameras. "He is going to die!"

I have no sympathy for Timothy McVeigh. I am appalled at his crime. But I am equally appalled at the unrestrained sense of glee that has come over so many people at the sentence of death now imposed upon him. Try as I might I can find no sensible reason for society to kill him. To condemn him to life in prison without possibility of parole would be a much better sentence.

It certainly is not for punishment. A quick painless death is going to be much easier than fifty years of life behind prison walls. To have to get up each day knowing where he is and why he is there, to watch the country he supposedly loved and wanted to defend move on without him, to become middle-aged and old while alone, knowing he was still the object of scorn — this would be true punishment for his crime.

Killing him is not a deterrent to violence. No one who would consider doing what he did would find a quick and painless death as the possible punishment a reason to cease plans for such destruction. Capital punishment has never been proven to be a deterrent to crime.

His death by lethal injection is not to save money. Between now and the time he will die more dollars will be spent on him than it would cost to lock him up and throw away the key.

The supposed reason given by some of the relatives of the victims who want him dead is so that "we can put all of this behind us and go on with our lives". It is a myth that killing Timothy McVeigh will heal the survivors of their grief. I have spent hundreds of hours with people who have lost loved ones, sometimes through violent crime, and I have never known the death of the perpetrator to solve anything or heal anyone.

But many of the gleeful people rejoicing in the death sentence don't know anyone from Oklahoma City and have no wounds to heal. Why do they want him dead? What is there about society killing one of us that is so appealing to others?

We say we kill criminals because of the crime that has been committed. We say it is punishment. We say it is the only way to keep society safe. We say that killing this particular criminal means he or she will never commit that crime again. We say it will deter others.

But I think the real reasons are much less noble. I think we sanction and encourage state killing because parts of us are still barbarian. American society has low regard for human life in general, one night of television news and entertainment proves that. The right to be alive is no longer absolute, but is becoming increasingly relative. To be alive one must be "convenient", "wanted", "useful", "healthy". Death is "no big deal", with some of us even claiming that there is a "duty to die."

Timothy McVeigh will probably die. It will not be for four or five years, with millions of dollars, hours of television coverage, and miles of newsprint devoted to him between now and then. When he does die there will be live coverage of it from outside the prison walls, probably with the big anchors themselves jockeying for position.

He and his crime will dominate our lives much more than if he had been locked up forever. His life between now and then will be busy, filled with endless legal happenings. He will probably never have the time in solitude and pain to repent of his sins and come to terms with God.

But his death is what society wants. When Timothy McVeigh dies we will all be informed that we now feel better because he is dead, we will be encouraged to share in the glee of the woman in the yellow dress and savor the moment of the execution — because that's what real Americans do.

July 25, 1997

Integrity Is The Basis For Happiness

Some time ago a young man running for a major political office in a potentially ugly election came to me for some advice. I told him to sit down and write out his moral position on life, clearly articulating the consistent principles by which he made his decisions. He couldn't do it — he lost the election.

What he could not do was find any consistent principles which govern his actions. It is not that he did not have some principles, but rather that the principles he had were not consistent, not logical, and certainly not mutually compatible.

My young friend is not alone. There are people who have consistent principles and struggle to live up to them, and there are people who have no principles at all. But there are many people, maybe most people in our culture, who have a buffet line of incompatible principles by which they try to live. My old aunt used to describe men like this as "jerks who think they can fool around but then insist on marrying a virgin."

Moral consistency is having the various principles by which we make decisions fit together. There can be negative moral consistency, such as the person who only cares about himself or herself in every situation. But here I am talking about positive moral consistency, which we also call "moral integrity".

Consistency or integrity means that we do not make decisions about each and every situation independently, but rather that there is a foundation from which our decisions come. For example a person who has the foundational principle that stealing is wrong, does not steal even if to do so would be easy. Another example would be the person who believes in the sanctity of marriage does not commit adultery even if there is no danger of getting caught.

But having a disconnected series of principles is not enough to be a person of integrity, those principles must fit together and be consistent. We know what consistency is when we see it.

Someone who says and does the same thing appeals to us as a person of integrity.

We also can easily see hypocrisy when it shows up in the people around us. We are slower to see it in ourselves or in the groups we belong to.

Many of modern America's difficulties with consistency and integrity revolve around the issue of life. Neither political party has any integrity or consistency on any life issues including abortion, capital punishment, euthanasia, aid to the poor, etc. Individual candidates pander to the crowds by picking a position on each issue by checking the polls.

This was well exemplified by the northwest senator who for years called himself "pro-life" because he said he opposed abortion, but he voted for every bomb, every execution, every cut in aid to the poor. The man was not pro-life but anti-life. The man was a hypocrite, but got elected over and over.

Hypocrisy is an expensive habit, its price is peace of mind and joy of heart. Hypocrisy is tolerated in politicians and pushy business types, most of whom are unhappy, driven people. Hypocrisy lays waste to marriages, families, personal satisfaction.

Integrity brings peace of mind and joy of heart, a sense of tranquility in the center of the soul. But it takes work to acquire integrity. It takes asking oneself deep disturbing questions and forcing out the answers. Questions such as: "What is the difference between killing a baby just after birth and aborting a baby before birth?" or "If suicide for some people is going to be OK, why not for all people? Why can't doctors kill anyone who wants to be killed?" or "If we feed the hungry at all, should it be all the hungry or just the deserving hungry?"

The coming Oregon public debate about suicide and mercy killing should force all of us to examine ourselves to discover: 1) if we have any foundational principles, and 2) if so, are these principles consistent?

To begin the self review I suggest a discussion around the dinner table about this question: "America says killing is wrong. How is that principle consistent with aborting babies, executing by state order people who have committed crimes, and killing off old and sick people?"

August 29, 1997

Do Inconvenient People Have Any Value?

Not too long after the Madison family moved into the mobile home park the manager dropped by to see them.

After the initial pleasantries he got to the point of his visit. "I would like you to think about perhaps moving on to another mobile home park. I'm not sure this is the right place for you."

"Is there a problem? I really do try to keep everything clean and nice," Mrs. Madison asked in a sweet voice. She knew the real reason, and she wanted the manager to admit it, put it into real words.

"Oh no, there is no problem like that at all. It's . . . it's . . . your son. He makes some of the other people who live here uncomfortable. Now I want you to understand he is fine with me, and I have no problem with retarded people, but there are people who do."

"Jake is not retarded, Mr. Armbruster, he has Down's Syndrome. It is a very different thing."

"Well, I don't care what he has. You two are fine people, but he . . um . . . he looks different. I don't want people to see him and think that is the type of people who live here.

"Now I know I can't make you move, all of these new laws make sure of that. But I think you understand my position. Your son is inconvenient and we just can't have him around here."

The manager had finally used the magic word, the new description of the unwanted people in our society. Each age has had its outcasts, its people that were forced to the fringe or beyond. In America of the 1990's the outcasts are <u>inconvenient</u>.

Convenient people are those we like to have around us. They are the beautiful, the witty, the clever, the powerful, the bright, the wealthy, and all the people who aspire to be those things. Inconvenient people are those we do not like around us. Inconvenient people are not usually pretty, they are often poor, and they are sometimes not very bright.

26

The value of people in our culture comes from the amount they contribute to society. Convenient people contribute so they have value. Inconvenient people are accused of not contributing so they lack value. The old, the poor, the mentally incompetent, the lame, the blind, the deaf — these people do not have value.

Imagine being told that not just your presence but your very existence is inconvenient. That is increasingly happening to the elderly members of our society. Insurance companies are saying that too many people are living too long — thus profits are dropping. It is inconvenient for insurance companies to have so many old people. It is inconvenient for many children to have to take care of an aged parent. It is inconvenient in a time of shrinking tax dollars to take money that could be used for the young, and waste it on the old who are only going to die eventually anyway. Writers are speaking of a "responsibility to die."

Our society is efficient. Inconvenient people are being gotten rid of. The inconvenience of an unwanted pregnancy is solved by aborting the inconvenient fetus. Inconvenient convicted criminals are being killed faster than ever, because keeping them in jail for life is just a waste of money. Having to feed them, house them, take care of them is inconvenient.

Physician assisted suicide is one of the first steps in getting rid of the inconvenient old people. Right behind it is physician assisted "life termination" for the inconvenient in comas, those who cannot recover, and those whose minds are gone. A son or daughter will say, "Mother would never have wanted to live like this, Doctor, let's do her in." With that, the inconvenient parent will cease to live. After that more and more categories of inconvenient people will be added to those who will be terminated.

I am afraid of becoming inconvenient. It could well be the end of me. My father's five years of living with Alzheimer's may not be a luxury that I will be given if the disease comes to me. There are those who have publicly stated that Alzheimer's patients should be terminated because they are a waste of precious resources. Those resources should be saved for the people who have value, the people who are convenient.

Mrs. Madison says that she read the Old Testament for years and saw all those passages where God tells the Hebrew people to take care of the orphans, widows, and foreigners among them. But those passages never meant anything until she realized that those people were the inconvenient people of that era. God is speaking to us now through those people and those texts. God is telling us again that human value comes from just being, not from what we do, but from who we are.

By the way, the Madisons refused to move, and the owner tormented them. Then another family moved in with a blind child, and third family with a young girl in a wheelchair. The owner sold the mobile home park and moved away.

The Death Of Diana, Princess Of Wales

At first the hotel room television made no sense. It was early Sunday morning in London, and gradually I realized that the commentators were talking about the death of Diana, Princess of Wales, in a Paris car crash the night before. We who were visiting from Central Oregon were soon to share with the British people one of the most profound weeks of their modern history.

I have lived in England, but nothing had prepared me for the depth of feeling, the overwhelming grief, the enormity of the public demonstrations that came in wave after wave, day by day, each event an ever more powerful sign of devotion for Diana. The city stopped, the country stopped, as millions of flowers were laid in places of remembrance in every little town and village as well as at all the major sites. Over a thousand books of condolences were filled with letters and poetry to the princess, written by men and women who had waited for up to eleven hours in chilly weather.

The media coverage focused on the events of the life and tragic death of the princess, with few reporters willing to delve into the meaning of that life, and especially into the meaning of her death. But it was the little that was said about meaning that had the most effect on me.

In Britain, like Oregon, most people do not go to church, attendance is among the lowest in Europe. While many of the 55 million British people are nominally Anglicans, less than a million of these attend church. The most active religions in Britain are Roman Catholic, Moslem, and Hindu, but the overall numbers of all of these are still small. Many observers call Britain a "post Christian" country. A very large number of people say they do not believe in God and have no religious faith at all.

Because of this lack of religious faith getting people on the street to speak about the <u>meaning</u> of life and the <u>meaning</u> of death was extremely difficult. Even the famous funeral had little religious content and almost no mention of the Resurrection and life everlasting. A woman on the street when asked how she responded when her daughter asked where Diana was now, said she had no answer — "Diana was a shooting star that came and went."

Many people said that Diana would live on in the good work she had done, but the thought that she herself would live on in a resurrection was absent from their thoughts. Two people quoted the line, "Life sucks and then you die." Much of the public grief had a decided tinge of despair and pessimism, that inability of people without faith to find any meaning in death.

There was a noticeable difference when the interviewed people proclaimed themselves as having faith. They saw meaning in Diana's life, in her struggles to overcome her eating disorder, her failed marriage, her efforts to raise her sons, and the example she was of someone trying to better the world. But they also saw Diana as someone blessed by God, a God who now would reward her for all she had done.

The people of faith saw her life as changed not ended, while the people without faith saw it as simply over. Those with faith could explain death to their children with optimism and joy, those without faith were always at a loss for words.

One image that struck me deeply was a young man placing one more bouquet on the enormous mound in front of Kensington Palace. When asked why he did so he simply said he wanted to do something for Princess Diana and didn't know what else to do. When asked if he was also praying for her he looked confused and surprised: "I don't really know what prayer is or how to do it, or why." Then he added, "I think I'll just go home and get drunk."

Without God life and death make no sense, have no meaning. With God they are wonderful beautiful mysteries. May our loving God grant peace and eternal rest to Diana, Princess of Wales, and let perpetual light shine upon her. May she rest in peace. Amen.

October 31,1997

Christian Churches Compelled To Be Counter-Cultural

One of the major reasons Jesus Christ was executed was his public rejection of much of the culture of his society. It has been said [especially in the Gospels of Matthew and Mark] that he sealed his fate when he did what a Jewish man was not supposed to do — spoke with and then cured a Syro-Phoenician woman.

Being "counter-cultural" is an essential aspect of being Christian. It is the point of tension, the spark, the catalyst that has identified vibrant Church life for the past two thousand years.

"Counter-cultural" means believing and living in ways that go against the normal, the usual, the accepted, the expected ways of the society or culture. It is "living in the world but not of the world." It is one of the most difficult aspects of being a follower of Jesus.

The first level of difficulty is determining when the demands of the Gospel are in conflict with the norms of society. When cultural values were blatantly anti-gospel, as in Roman society, the conflict was obvious. But ever since the Emperor Constantine adopted Christianity as the official religion, it has been difficult to differentiate Christian values from social values. Sometimes it is hard to see that something everyone accepts as normal and even good is, in reality, contrary to the teachings of Christ. Slavery, racism, child labor, militarism, corporate greed, gender discrimination are only a few historical examples.

When a societal or cultural value is seen as opposed to the Gospel, the second level of difficulty is determining what if anything can or should be done about it. Usually good Christians just live personally rejecting the evil value, but not actively working against it. But when that evil value threatens people, especially the weak and inconvenient, then Christianity comes into open conflict with society.

In America the tensions between the culture and Christianity have carved a wide swath through our history and our society. It was the counter-cultural beliefs and practices of religion that forced the Pilgrims and Puritans to move to New England, that encouraged the Mormons to go to Utah, that created the Catholic School system, that led clergy of every denomination to protest the Vietnam War, and that inspired Martin Luther King to have a dream.

But when Churches failed to confront societal values that threatened the weak and inconvenient, values which were in conflict with the Gospel, society, the culture, and the Church all suffered. Denominations split during the civil war; religious leaders did not protest the incarceration of the Japanese-Americans during World War II; many Protestant denominations did not denounce the Ku Klux Klan as it persecuted blacks, Jews and Catholics.

Rarely in American history have the tensions between Christianity and society been as high as right now. Almost every denomination of Christians is struggling with the challenges of determining the Christian stance on various aspects of the ever-changing American society. Homosexuality, war, the environment, abortion, land mines, physician-assisted suicide, gender bias, pre-marital sex, tobacco, drugs, euthanasia, immigration, welfare reform — this is only a partial list of issues on which society and the gospel are often at odds. How to respond to these issues is a major focus of every Christian Church in America today.

The tensions caused by Christian opposition to cultural values can lead to religious bigotry. Non-religious people often object to and even ridicule the involvement of Churches in social issues. Often showing a shocking ignorance of Christianity's essential responsibility to be counter-cultural, modern merchants of culture want people of religion to be quiet when faced with values and customs contrary to the Gospel. When people of religion are not quiet, these critics often resort to bigotry and prejudice against the religion, rather than debate the issues. The most recent and most blatant American examples of this are unfortunately here in Oregon.

Hindsight and a look at other countries tells us that the German Churches did not do enough to oppose Hitler and National Socialism, that the Dutch Churches did not do enough to combat early attacks on the sanctity of life, and that the Argentine Churches did not reject the culture of militarism that created the times of great horror. Whenever the Christian Churches cease to critique and if necessary oppose the values of society, the results to all people are catastrophic.

Thus all Christian Churches will continue to try to live up to the essence of the faith, to know and understand the true values of God, and to work to protect weak and inconvenient people from a culture that does not want them to exist. Christianity by its essence is counter-cultural. It is always looking for a Syro-Phoenician woman to speak to.

Church of St. Edward the Martyr

November 28, 1997

True Human Freedom Comes From Thankfulness

When the first fire destroyed their home, I was just in high school. When the second fire cost them both the new home and severely burned their daughter, I was in college. The boating accident that cost the life of their son was just after I was ordained.

Both are living with cancer, and the financial loss from being swindled by a business partner has left them with almost no money.

Approaching the house on the tiny sidewalk that connected their "tiny bit of heaven" to the outside world, I am overwhelmed with a sense of peace and serenity. Visiting Madge and Darian is always a pleasant experience. I have known them for years, first as younger friends of my parents', then as older friends of mine.

What makes the visit to their home such a delight is the wonderful optimistic vision of life that both of them exude. It is not that they are pollyanna people, it is not that they live in a fantasy world. They speak of their dead son and their permanently scarred daughter. They laugh about the use the business partner made of their money in the high life of Hawaii. They talk openly about the almost certainty of their deaths by cancer.

What sets Madge and Darian apart is that each of them individually and both of them together are truly free. They view everything that exists as gifts from God to be savored, enjoyed, and used well. But nothing except their relationship with God is permanent.

They truly loved their son Bob. His loss was deeply painful, but not an angry despairing type of pain. Rather it was a loving poignant type of pain, the pain of loss firmly planted on the foundation of faith. Each mention of Bob begins with an acknowledgement of the thanks they give God for the gift of their son. They wish his time with them had been longer, but they also give thanks that they will join Bob in heaven someday.

We've talked about their attitude, their ability to be so calm and peaceful in the face of so much adversity. They willingly admit that achieving that peace has not been easy.

For them, the key decision of all life is the decision to acknowledge that we stand in a relationship of thankfulness to God. Once each one of us individually and as couples or families can establish that relationship of thankfulness, then all the pieces of life fit together. In relationship with God, they found true human freedom.

They can absorb the accidents, diseases, and even sins that life brings to them because their foundation is not in the world. They are free because their foundation is in their relationship with God. Everything in this world, even their children, are gifts from God to be cared for and enjoyed. Thanking God for these gifts establishes that foundation.

They believe that God gave them the gifts, they do not believe that God took the gifts away. God allowed accident, disease, or sin to take the gifts away, and God mourned with them their loss. He also gave them the grace to endure the loss.

What keeps them from being sickeningly sweet, yucky people is the way they thank God. As Darian says, it is sometimes easy to thank him, but usually it takes work. It takes being angry at him first for allowing the pain, and then time to overcome the desire for self-pity or revenge. Only after some real work can true thanks begin. But when it does, the peace and joy it brings is truly awesome. At that point they become free.

These people are incredibly mentally healthy, a health that comes from a lifetime of thanking God for all that is. I cannot help but compare their attitude to that of people who moan and groan about the difficulties of life, or people who hold grudges against imagined or even real hurts, or people who live for revenge or wallow in self-pity.

What makes Madge and Darian so healthy is that they thank God for each day and everything they have. They teach me the meaning of thanks, of thanksgiving, and of Thanksgiving Day. The only source of true personal human freedom is giving thanks to God.

December 26,1997

Hidden Out There In The Holly

The man came into the empty church before Mass on a cold December Saturday evening. No one was there to see him put the pills into his mouth or slink slowly down between the pews. When the people found him it was too late, he was dead. To this day no one knows his name.

I was pastor of the parish where that man killed himself fourteen years ago. He is always on my mind in the season of Christmas. I remember and pray for him. But I also remember and pray for the many other people who find this the most difficult time of the year.

"Joy to the World" . . . "Peace on earth and goodwill to all" . . . "O come all ye faithful" – we are told from childhood that Christmas is the great time of joy and happiness. We religious leaders stress the love of God and the fellowship of all people. We speak of giving, generosity, thankfulness, and human goodness.

The commercial culture tells us that we deserve the best from Santa, which means that it should be purchased from the best stores. We are taught to judge the sincerity of the giver by the price of the gift. Television tells us that real people, good people, normal people, the people we really want to be, always go out to dinner with friends, or have endless holiday parties with marvelous foods. They all have happy well adjusted families, and live in beautiful houses where candles always burn and the television is never on.

None of us measure up to either the religious or the commercial ideal set before us. Most of us adjust to the contradictions between that ideal and our own reality. But some people cannot make that adjustment. For them, Christmas is the time of failure, pain, suffering, loneliness, and deep depression.

I once knew a lady whose childhood memories of Christmas centered around her drunken father tearing apart the Christmas tree, using its branches to beat her mother. I knew a man whose mother committed suicide on Christmas eve because she had no money for gifts for her children. There is the man whose wife left him ON Christmas eve to marry her boss, taking his children with her. She spends Christmas surrounded by rich splendor – he is always alone for the holidays.

Each sad person has his or her own story, and unless the story touches Christmas, most people will find a sympathetic ear.. But stories of people who hate Christmas, or find December the worst month of the year, or suffer deep debilitating depression have no listeners. We "normal people" don't want to listen because we don't want our own Christmas ruined by someone else's tale of woe. We will give to the family without heat and to the children without presents [although usually from a safe distance so their poverty will not personally affect us], but we avoid the sad, lonely, depressed people altogether.

And the sad, lonely, depressed people try very hard to hide their sadness, loneliness, and depression because society says – and religion says – that people have no right to be sad during Christmastime. When someone who hates the holidays hears that a good Christian should be filled with joy and happiness at the birth of Christ, then the conclusion is obvious. When a depressed mother doesn't want to make cookies or decorations, she must be a bad mother. For sad depressed people the holidays become a downhill spiral of constantly failed expectations, and bouts of isolation and anxiety.

The commercial side of Christmas is not going to do anything about bringing some type of peace and healing to the people who find Christmas difficult, that is beyond the concerns of the marketplace. But the people who live with Christmas pain should be a central focus of the religious world. No just from those of us who preach from holiday pulpits, but from those who sit in the pews. All of us must learn to see, hear, feel, notice, and care about those around us who find Christmas hard to live through.

We must become the listeners, taking that risk of personal involvement which marks true Christian endeavors. And when we respond we must help people lower their expectations, live within their abilities, and have the freedom to dislike Christmas. Most sad, lonely, depressed people at Christmas need only to be hugged, cared about, and listened to – they don't need to be "cured". Their sadness usually has a history and richness that each person has to live with. Our roles as the people who love them, is to let them know they are loved even as they live through their sadness .

When it came time to bury the man who died in our church, hundreds of people came to the funeral, held just a day or two after Christmas. I preached that all of us, without judgement, had to care about the sad people of Christmastime. Afterwards a lady I had never seen before came up and spoke to me. "Thank you, Father. I dread Christmas. For a variety of personal reasons I hate this season of the year. But now for the first time I have heard my pain acknowledged in Church. There are many of us who feel that way, hidden out there in the holly."

January 24, 1998

Christians United And Yet Divided

When I was little, a kid named Calvin came up to three or four of us coming home from Catholic school.

"My Sunday school teacher said you Catholics don't believe in the Bible and you're all goin' to hell."

"We do believe in the Bible. Besides all you Protestants are goin' to hell because you're not in the true Church," Molly said. She was an excellent spokesperson.

"You don't believe in the Bible. You don't believe in the Bible." He sang a sing-song chant as we tried to walk away from him. It only ended when Molly decked him with a right hook. Calvin's family moved away not too long after that.

Times have changed. January 18 — 25 is now the "Week of Prayer for Christian Unity." All Christians are urged to pray for each other and for mutual understanding. Mutual understanding must be based on honest efforts to understand those areas where Christians agree, as well as those areas where we do not.

The Bible is a subject about which there is much agreement and some fundamental disagreement. While all true Christians believe the Bible to be the inspired Word of God, they differ in how to explain what that means, and in how to acquire that inspiration. It is always a source of confusion and wonder to Christians and non-Christians how and why people who claim to believe in the same God and the same Son of God have different understandings of the Bible.

While it is difficult to simplify the differences, there are two major areas about which there are major disagreements in understandings of the scriptures. The first of these is the relationship between the Bible and the Church; the second is how to read and understand the Bible.

Some Churches, my own included, understand the Bible, especially the New Testament, to be the "Holy Book of the Church". We see the New Testament as the story of the early Church's self-understanding. Jesus first founded the Church. Then, inspired by God, the New Testament arose out of the Church. Likewise the Old Testament arose from the chosen people of God as they were inspired to write their own story.

Other Churches see the Church as arising out of the Bible. The Bible becomes the rule or scale against which the Church and all other aspects of Christian living are to be measured. To these Christians the Bible is not the book of the Church, rather the Church has to be the "Church of the Holy Book".

The implications of these two starting points are great. Those who believe that the Bible arises out of the Church give a great importance to the meaning of "Church". They believe that tradition and the development of doctrine are sources of revelation, knowledge and practice that expand on and sometimes explain the Bible. These religions stress the mystical body of Christ and the interdependence of believers. These denominations are many of the liturgical Churches including the Catholics, the Orthodox, and some of the mainline Protestant bodies.

Those denominations which see the Church arising from the Bible stress the personal salvation of each believer. They believe that the only real source of knowledge of God is the Bible itself. Thus all aspects of the life of a Christian must be compared to the Bible for legitimacy. These denominations often advertise themselves as "Bible based".

The differences in understandings means that things found in the tradition of some of the liturgical churches, for example the sacraments, the rosary, holy water, or icons, are rejected by others as not being found in the Bible. It often means that Christians have a very difficult time even talking to each other. In time of ugliness one group says that the other "worships the Church instead of God"; while the second group contents that the other "worships the Bible instead of God."

The second major difference falls along roughly the same denominational lines. Some, including my own, believe that the Bible must be understood "contextually," which means that each passage must be understood in context, with the where, when, how of the work being totally understood. The reader does not seek meaning word for word or line by line.

The second group of Churches believe that Scripture must be

understood literally, which means taking each word and each line to mean exactly what they say. Some literalists are more demanding than others, but almost all believe that in "God's Word" each word must be seen as being put into the text for a specific reason.

These differences mean that literalists and contextualists usually have difficulty speaking with each other. One mentions a bible verse and thinks the meaning is self-evident [e.g. John 3/16]. The other understands nothing from just one verse and needs the entire Gospel of John to understand what is being said. Members of contextual religions see no need to memorize Bible texts or know Bible verses. Members of literal religions often know hundreds of Bible passages by heart.

Most people wish that Christianity could someday come together into one large happy family. I frankly doubt if that will ever happen. The enormity of the revelation of God contained in scripture can never be easily or completely understood by people. Thus there will always be various ways to understand the message of Christ. Each group thinks that its way is correct. I personally think my religious tradition is correct, that is why I find it easy to believe as a Roman Catholic.

But I, and all Christians, have an obligation to understand why there are differences between Christians. In this week of Christian unity, we acknowledge that one thing we can do is pray together and for each other. What we are coming to understand is that in the end, Molly's arm and Calvin's jaw belong to children of the same God.

February 20, 1998

Ash Wednesday, Publicly Professing Sin And Hope

The ice cold wind cut like a knife through their thin tunics. The sinners — Gustav, Mongo, Bernice — stood shivering on the steps as the cathedral door slowly creaked open. The townsfolk waited as the bishop listened as each one confessed, loud enough for all to hear.

Gustav had killed his wife and child in a drunken rage. Mongo had stolen cattle from a farmer and gold from the king. Bernice had murdered her neighbor by poisoning the well. The penance pronounced by the bishop on that Shrove ["to clean"] Tuesday in 620 AD in a town in northern France was the same: public ashes, forty days of fasting to be spent living on the steps of the church, and no admittance into Mass until absolution which would be given on Holy Thursday. The ashes would be poured all over their bodies the next morning, the first day of Lent, appropriately called Ash Wednesday.

Two hundred years later not just the major sinners but the minor ones as well privately confessed their sins to the priest on Shrove Tuesday. Each person was given a penance, and after promising to do the penance, each was given private absolution. They returned to their homes to use up the last of the eggs, butter, cheese, meat, and oil, making this a "Fat Tuesday" or "Mardi Gras." None of these foods could be eaten during the Lenten fast.

On the next day, Ash Wednesday, ashes were poured on the heads of all the people, major sinners and minor sinners alike. The beginning of the modern Ash Wednesday had begun.

Today in the liturgical churches [Catholic, Lutheran, Orthodox, Episcopal, etc.] these customs endure. While Shrove Tuesday has lost the element of confession of sins but strongly retains the idea of Mardi Gras, Ash Wednesday has continued as the beginning of a time of reflection and penance, a time of preparing for the coming triumph of Easter.

Because Easter is the most important Christian feast, the time

42

after Easter had always been celebrated for forty days or even fifty days until Ascension Thursday and Pentecost. Lent began as a time of reflection on the days before Easter, Holy Saturday, Good Friday, and Holy Thursday. It gradually extended into forty days, the mythical number so often used in the Bible to mean a special amount of time.

As the Roman empire fell into disarray and lawlessness and sin became more common, the forty days before Easter began to be seen as the time when sin needed to be faced and overcome. At first it was the most visible great sins of only a few, but eventually it became obvious that all people needed to do something to overcome their own sinfulness. All had to get ready for Easter by confession, penance, and absolution. The sign of the commitment to do this was to be marked by ashes.

Today most Catholics and many members of the other liturgical churches go to church on Ash Wednesday and have the mark of ashes made on their foreheads. Even a few years ago most people washed the ashes off before going to work, but now more and more people are leaving them visible all day as a sign of both their own personal sinfulness and the hope of forgiveness and salvation. The reception of ashes is a mark of taking responsibility for one's own actions, for one's own sins, for one's own need for life everlasting.

The reception of ashes on Ash Wednesday is open to anyone and everyone. In Catholic churches both Catholics and non-catholics, christians and non-christians, in large numbers, come forward on that day to admit publicly that he or she has sinned and desires the forgiveness and understanding of God.

And Lent, those forty special days of seeking that forgiving and understanding God, is a time open to everyone as well, each in his or her own way.

This year Ash Wednesday is February 25th.

March 27, 1998

How Do Churches View Role Of The Individual Person?

In one of my recent column I discussed the difference in the way various Christian Churches understand the scriptures, and why Christians at the Catholic end of the spectrum view and use the Bible so differently from those at the fundamentalist end of the spectrum. I have been asked if in future columns I would explain the differences in others areas of Christian belief. Today I will do so in the understanding of "Church."

One of the truly great and major differences between Catholic theology [as well as the Orthodox] and classic fundamentalist theology is the understanding of the role of the individual person. Catholic and Orthodox theology puts great emphasis on "humanity," on "community," on the "people of God," while classic fundamentalist theology puts great emphasis on the "individual person," on "personal acceptance," on "personal salvation." Not all modern Protestant Churches hold as strongly to individualism as classic fundamentalism does. The various Protestant denominations have taken theological positions along a line between greater emphasis on the community and greater emphasis on the individual. To a large extent what each Christian denomination understands "Church" to be depends on where on this spectrum that denomination falls.

For Catholics, each person is born in need of the grace of Jesus Christ [the Catholic emphasis of the doctrine of Original Sin]. God's grace in baptism not only brings the person being baptised into a personal relationship with God, but essential to this relationship is the fact that the person comes into the family of Christ, into the People of God, into the Church. Catholics see each person as having an individual relationship with God which is essentially interconnected with his or her equally important relationship with God in and through the Church. While distinct these relationships cannot be separated. Equally important each individual is interconnected with each and with all other individuals as the Church.

The best analogy to understand the Catholic viewpoint would be children belonging to a family. Each child has 1) a relationship with the parent, but each is also part of 2) the relationship of all the children with the parent. Going further, each child has 3) a relationship with each of the other children and 4) all the other children together. The family may be good, bad, dysfunctional, excellent or whatever – but it is still that person's family and gives that person his or her identity.

That is what happens to a person spiritually in Baptism – he or she becomes the Church. He or she does not "join" the Church like joining a club. He or she becomes the Church and that gives the person his or her identity.

One of the effects for the person who becomes the Church, is that the grace of God comes to each person not only directly from God, but also through the other people who are the Church. Each person's relationship with God is both direct and indirect, both with God as an individual and with God through other people. People who live with the grace of God can share that grace with others. This includes the dead as well as the living, which explains why saints are so important in this understanding of Church.

The classic fundamentalist understanding of Church is almost totally different. It has a much greater emphasis on the individual. Each person is born in sin [the fundamentalist emphasis of the doctrine of Original Sin]. Baptism washes away that sin, and gives each person an individual relationship with God. Each person has to come to personal terms with his or her relationship with God, by making an individual commitment, an individual personal act of acceptance of Jesus Christ as Lord and Savior. In some denominations individuals can state the date and place where he or she was "saved."

In fundamentalist theology Church then is the name for the gathering of those people who have accepted Jesus Christ, who have been baptised and saved. Each has his or her personal relationship with God. Each person has God's grace. Each person can encourage others, can pray with others, can pray for others, can be joyful that other individuals have a personal relationship with God, can rejoice that other individuals have been saved. But no individual can actually share God's grace with another individual.

Christian denominations or churches are groupings of people

who give effective encouragement and support to an individual person's relationship with God. Individuals join the denomination or church in which they find support. If that encouragement weakens, the person must move on to a different denomination, because it really does not make a difference what denomination a person belong to as long as that denomination gives support and encouragement, and fits the individual's definition of Christian.

Each individual must live out his or her commitment each day, each minute. What this means in specific terms is determined by reading, studying, praying with the Bible. By joining with other Bible-based Christians each individual can both know how to live, and create a society where Bible values are paramount. In all of this other people can support an individual's relationship with God, but cannot effect that relationship, because people cannot actually share God's grace with each other.

These two views of "Church" are truly different. Catholicism is a "community religion" where the community of faith is as important as the individual's faith. Protestantism in general and fundamentalist Protestantism in particular is an "individual religion" where the individual faith of the person is all important. It is this difference that lies at the heart of why Catholics must be married in the Catholic Church, why Catholics must go to Mass on Sunday, why only Catholics can receive communion at Mass, why the Pope and saints are of such high value. It is this difference that explains why fundamentalists speak about "being saved," why Baptism is the only sacrament, and why communion is only a memorial of Christ. And it is this difference that explains why other Protestant Churches fall somewhere in between the Catholics and the fundamentalists.

April 24, 1998

Is Religion For Stability Or Is Religion For Change?

One of the great conflicts in the world of religion casts on one side those people who want religion to be the great source of stability and constancy for the world. These people, found in every religious tradition and denomination, are determined to use faith in God as the foundation for a stable society, the font of unchanging values. I do not want to use the word "conservative" to describe them because that word has so much political baggage connected to it, but they often use it to describe themselves. I will call them "stabalists".

On the other side of this debate are those people who want religion to be the source of inspiration and progress. These people, also present throughout the religious spectrum, see faith in God as the font of new and constantly changing challenges to the here and now. They call for religion to "comfort the afflicted and afflict the comfortable." I do not use the word "liberal" for them, and neither do they, but those who oppose them call them liberals because that word has become the highest religious insult possible. I will call them "changists".

This conflict between those using religion as the source of stability and those using religion as the source of change becomes apparent in issues such as abortion, homosexuality, divorce and remarriage, forgiveness of sins, service to the poor, personal accountability, capital punishment, school prayer, ecumenism, and many other topics.

The "stabalists" want to find one standard answer to each question, each issue, and simply announce that the topic has been permanently settled. For example, these people might say that abortion is wrong, homosexuality is wrong, school prayer is right, capital punishment is right, the poor should help themselves, etc. For any topic the requirement is to go back to the source of knowledge and determine the answer. For Catholic "stabilists" that source is usually what the tradition of the Church teaches, for fundamentalists it is what the

Bible teaches, for Muslims what the Koran says, for Jews the Torah. But once an answer to a social problem is found, that answer is set in concrete.

The "changists" simply do not find such permanent answers acceptable. They contend that because the world changes, and people change, the answers to questions must change as well. They believe that humanity is indeed progressing, a progress guided and inspired by God.

They are comfortable with saying that abortion may be wrong but in some cases it may be right, that homosexuality may be a legitimate life style, especially if homosexuality is genetic. They may hold that because only Protestant school prayer was allowed in the past, it did so much harm to Catholics and Jews that it should never be allowed again, and that capital punishment may have outlived any moral foundation it used to have.

These are very important issues in many denominations. The Baptists, Episcopalians, Presbyterians and others are very split on the issue of homosexuality. My own Catholic Church is headed for a major battle as the pope and the bishops of the world get ready to equate advocacy of capital punishment with advocacy for abortion as both morally wrong sins against life. Many American Catholic laymen and women are going to have great difficulty with that teaching, and many priests are going to be in the middle between the bishops and the people.

There is often a nostalgic element in the "stabalists" that yearns back to some Golden Age when life was easier. In Catholic "stabalists" there is this desire for it to be 1955 when Pius XII was Pope, Eisenhower was president, and no one had heard of Vatican II. Many others who want religion to provide stability also view the 1950's as much better than today.

Those advocating religion for change find this idea abhorrent. They view the 1950's as one of the most hypocritical and dishonest periods in American history, with racism, sexism, homophobia, and many other social evils publically tolerated in the name of stability. The only possible Golden Age for "changists" is in the future.

Is this conflict between the two parties solvable? Is there a way these two groups can live and work together in the same Church? I frankly am not sure they can, at least not without a great deal of work. And I doubt if that work will take place.

My pessimism came from the fact that solid core advocates of religion as stability have no desire to work with those advocating change. They view proponents of change as the enemy, and view even dialogue as requiring an openness to thinking differently, something they are not willing to do.

Advocates for change will talk to anyone anytime, that is essential to the mentality that a new thought, a new insight, might improve one's position. This very openness makes them appear to the other side as unstable, and therefore not worthy of discussion.

The only first step I can recommend is for each person to figure out where he or she is in this topic. Do you view religion as the source of stability or as the impetus for change? Has the Golden Age of religious values come and gone, and is it still in sight? Can values change or must they remain unchanging?

I have done this myself and I have helped others do it. What we all found out is that the answers have a great deal to do with who we understood God to be.

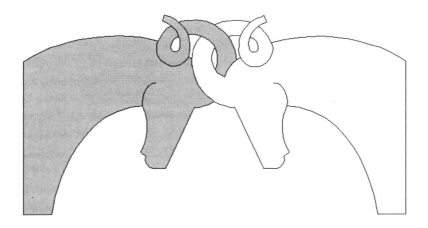

May 29, 1998

Sixty Four Shades Of Gray Apples And Oranges

Two friends of mine have not met, but they should. The first is a wonderful woman I used to work with who once insisted that the new fax machine must have "sixty four shades of gray." The second is a English clergyman who believes that the reason so many people have difficulty with strong religious morality, especially Catholic morality, is that the Church teaches in a manner that is "apples to most people's oranges."

They should meet because they are both people who appreciate the gray in a black and white world. They both know the difference between apples and oranges.

The moral tradition of the Catholic Church and much of Christianity comes from the Greek and Roman way of thinking and expressing important ideas. In this tradition the first step of teaching and understanding morality is the statement of a moral ideal as an absolute, a seemingly "non-negotiable" moral statement. Living up to this ideal is called "right" and violating this ideal is called "wrong." In this way of thinking the ideal, the absolute, does not change no matter what the circumstances are or what the local law may be.

The ideal does not change because in the second stage of teaching morality this absolute norm, this ideal, is brought into the realm of practical reality and appropriately adjusted. The norm remains absolute and the ideal remains unchanged, but in actual practice it is not totally lived up to.

"You shall not kill" is a good example. This is an absolute norm, and violating it is always "wrong". But we agree that in some situations, such as self-defense, killing might be justified. It is still "wrong" but the circumstances make it a "wrong" which is not a cause of guilt. It is an "OK wrong," which is very different from "right."

Another tradition of teaching or understanding morality comes from "enlightenment" thinking. In this style there is no ideal, no absolute, just practical rules for behavior. Morality and law reflect the pragmatic values of society at the time, and if times change the morality and law change as well. Sometimes it is society at large which makes morality; at other times it is sections of society that decide for themselves what is moral and what is not.

In this system "right" and "wrong" become very confusing terms. "Right" means something is permitted, and "wrong" means something is not. What is "right" or "wrong" changes constantly. Thus in America abortion, adultery, living together, same gender sexual activity, physician assisted suicide, are all "right" things to do because they are permitted. On the other hand, smoking, flirting, and prayer in schools are "wrong" because they are not permitted.. In this moral system everything is black or white – but the colors reverse fairly often.

When someone who is very comfortable with enlightenment morality hears someone talk who comes from Greco-Roman morality, he or she often gets angry. The Greco-Roman says "abortion is wrong" or "adultery is wrong" while the enlightenment says "abortion isn't wrong, it's right because it's legal," or "adultery isn't wrong, it right because most people today accept it." The end result is that people talk past each other, each incapable of understanding how the other could possibly believe what he or she said. They are apples and oranges.

Morality gets complicated even more when people who believe in absolutes and ideals fail to move to the second level of adjusting those ideals to a practical situation. They do this because they view adjusting absolutes or ideals to be a compromise, a cop-out. They argue, "How can it be an absolute if there are times when it doesn't apply?" The answer is that there are some things we do that are "wrong" yet doing that thing is the best we can do. That does not make it "right," it means it is "OK wrong," or wrong without the person being morally responsible for the wrong.

Odd as it may sound, the absolute world of Greco-Roman morality has the sixty four shades of gray. The ideal may be white, but few if any of us totally achieve the ideal, we all live in varying degrees of effort and success. But the existence of the ideal, the absolute, at least gives us a direction to head for, it gives us something to strive for.

The black and white world of enlightened morality is a circular world of fads and fashions. This year it is OK to be homosexual, next year it may not be. For awhile alcohol was forbidden in the USA now it is not. Enlightened morality has no foundation other than popular opinion and has no direction other that the whims of history.

I firmly believe in a morality with absolutes, with ideals, with direction. I often fail to live up to those ideals but at least I know where I am headed, and what I have to do to get there.

June 27, 1998

Healthy Religion Knows How To Laugh

Religion can take itself too seriously. It's an understandable temptation. When dealing with issues such as an omnipotent divinity, life, death, eternal glory, eternal punishment, and the ultimate meaning of life, it is easy to forget to laugh. But when religion forgets to laugh it begins to inaccurately reflect that omnipotent divinity and begins to distort that ultimate meaning of life.

There was a very wise old sister who became an official evaluator of convents and monasteries. She said she used two simple criteria to determine the overall health of a religious community. The first was looking at the cemetery because if Christian leaders do not take care of the dead they do not take care of the living. The second was asking if the leader of the community ever laughed, because a leader who does not laugh is leading people nowhere.

Laughter, humor and mirth are important elements of religion, especially the Christian religion. They are the external hallmarks of the great Christian virtue of joy, one of the essential characteristics of someone in union with God. If God lives within a religion or a person, there is joy. Joy is manifested by laughter, humor and mirth. There are of course other sources of external laughter besides internal joy, so not all laughter comes from God – but true joyful laughter does.

The virtue of joy is the most neglected of all the great manifestations of God's presence. Joy is more rare than humility, even more scarce than peace. Sober Christians have somehow connected sincerity with seriousness and joy with shallowness. A joyful priest or minister is viewed with suspicion, as someone who does not take the Gospel seriously. A joyful member of the laity can only be someone who really doesn't understand the depth of all Jesus had to say and teach, or worse still, someone who is unrepentant of his or her sins.

Joy gets such bad press because Christians equate [perhaps

not consciously] sin with pleasure. People often hear remarks such as "This is so much fun it must be sinful," as if physical or emotional pleasure cannot possibly be connected with something godly. Endure pain, quietly suffer and carry the cross – these are the things Christians are supposed to do, not have fun or laugh. To some, the Christian God has become an old bearded ogre in the sky keeping a record of every moment spent not being miserable, planning to punish people for those moments.

There really are Christians ministers who preach that kind of silly nonsense, but there are even more people who have fallen away from various churches who claim that is what they were taught either in Sunday school or parochial school. They claim that laughter and humor were viewed as sinful with the only mention of joy being the "joy of suffering" (whatever that is.) Often people who say such things make them up to justify their lack of church involvement, but the overall effect is to drive joy out of the popular image of religion.

Just because religion deals with serious issues does not mean it should be devoid of joy and humor. On the contrary, a church office should be a place where laughter is the most common sound, and where people obviously get pleasure from what they do. A church congregation should be joyful people who can see the presence of God in one another, and find joy in what they see. Priests and ministers should be transparent images of the joy of God – even while speaking about serious sin or grave temptation.

Not only is there no contradiction between feeling joy and being serious, on the contrary there is a vital connection. A person of joy can share God's joy with others, and in doing so show how all of those serious topics such as abortion, assisted suicide, other murders, rape, pillage, etc. are so very far from the joyful heart of God. It is difficult to recognize a joyless "hellfire and brimstone" preacher as having anything to do with the God most real Christian people have experienced and know. Those preachers make up their own God and Gospel to scare people into subjugation.

True Christianity lives in a preacher, a church, a congregation which deals with the serious topics but does so by inviting people to share in the joy of God by eliminating sin from their lives. There should be one person on every committee to hire every pastor and church employee whose only responsibility is to ask the question, "Do you know how to laugh and what makes you do so?" On the answer depends the whole law and the prophets – and the potential job.

Good religion is serious but joyful, not somber and depressing. Good Christians laugh. Good ministers and priests enjoy God. Good teaching has a sense of humor within it. Our good God has a sense of humor, how else could he have put up with us all of these years?

July 25, 1998

The Four Rights And Responsibilities Of Human Life

One of the basic realities of human life is the acknowledgment that there are some things which are right and some things which are wrong. Thousands of years of human thought have resulted in ethical and moral conclusions. For any moral conclusion to be accepted as truly describing real human life experience it must be seen as being consistent and having true integrity.

The fundamental Christian moral conclusions rest on the truth that there is a God who has created the world and all people. In that creation are certain human rights that express the inherent value of each person and all people. That value is prior to law, fundamental to law, and the criteria for law. The inherent value of each person and the rights that flow from that value also contain the responsibility for each person to exercise and protect those rights for themselves and for others. There are four interconnected inherent human rights and responsibilities contained in creation.

THE RIGHT TO BE BORN

Human life comes into being by the act of conception. From that moment onward each individual has the potential and the right to be born. Only by birth can a person have the opportunity to love and be loved, to dream, to do good for others, to accomplish, to become. The essence of being human is to be alive.

No human being is perfect, but each is unique. That lack of perfection does not cause a person to lose his or her right to be born. The unique individuality of each person, genetically and in all other ways, must not be sacrificed to create perfection.

THE RIGHT TO GROW

The human person is born and lives his or her entire life fragile and dependent — in need of others. Growth, which we acquire from other people, is the process by which additional life enters into a person. It is essential to being human that each person be given the necessities for growth, and that each person choose to grow. These essentials include the right to love, the right to worship, the right to food, the right to shelter, the right to learn, the right to medical care.

Each person has the right and corresponding responsibility to ensure that he or she exercises the right to grow and that all other people are given the same opportunity. Human beings are responsible for and accountable to one another.

THE RIGHT TO LIVE IN JUSTICE AND PEACE

Weak, strong, famous, unknown, rich, poor, gifted, disadvantaged — all people are unique manifestations of God's creative power. Each person has the right and corresponding responsibility to personally live in justice and peace and enable all others to do so as well.

Thus it is the responsibility of each individual and all of humanity to use the gifts of creation to overcome evil and promote goodness. It is one of the roles and obligations of government to be a mechanism by which this is done.

The offsprings of evil — drugs, terrorism, murder, violence, corruption, racism, sexism, persecution, and many others — must never be allowed to make victims of human beings. Each person has the right to live in a world of love, faith, hope, kindness, understanding, justice, and peace.

THE RIGHT TO DIE A NATURAL DEATH

Life is a mysterious gift from a God who loves and values each person. Life is intended to run its natural course. Death is not the ultimate evil, it is not the end of existence. Death is part of life, a most important and deeply sacred part of life.

Because we are interdependent and because we never cease to grow, no one, not even the individual nor the state, has sufficient reason to violate the right of a person to die a natural death. To deny anyone the opportunity to die when his or her time has come is to violate the meaning and purpose of why people were born, why they grow, why they live in justice and peace.

These four rights are from God. They are the foundation upon which Christianity bases its understanding of life and morality. The promotion of any one of them strengthens the rest, the violation of any weakens the remainder. It is the human challenge to live them fully.

August 28, 1998

Responsibility Includes The Consequences Of Actions

I raised a foster son. He was assigned to me by the courts when he was in his late teens, having grown up in a background of true neglect. One of our first major disagreements came when he did something wrong. It took awhile for him to even admit he had done it, but when he finally did I told him that his punishment was to be "grounded." He was totally amazed that he was going to be punished.

He argued with me: "I admitted I did it, that should be punishment enough. It happened four days ago. That was then and this is now. How can I be punished now for something that happened four days ago?"

He wasn't putting on an act. He truly had no concept of the consequences of an action. It took years for him to finally learn that every action, good or bad, has consequences, and the person who does that action is responsible for those consequences.

In all my years of working with youth I find that the absence of a sense of consequences is the most consistent difficulty many of them have with achieving maturity. Time after time young people do things, oblivious to the reality that there are consequences for what they are doing. I did a funeral for a kid killed when the car he was in crashed on the way back from a high school drinking party. The driver, totally drunk at the time, would not take responsibility for the death because his "intention was to get drunk and have a good time, not crash the car." All through the subsequent trial he could not understand why he should be held responsible for the consequences of getting drunk and driving a car when he didn't intend the accident to happen.

The task of teaching children the reality of consequences has become much more difficult by the unwillingness of the President of the United States to take responsibility for the consequences of his actions. His speech last week was almost exactly like my foster

59

son's years ago. He said he "takes full responsibility" for what he did and for misleading the American people. But in reality he has not taken responsibility, because to do so means dealing with the consequences of one's actions, and he has made no effort to acknowledge or deal with those consequences.

Leaving aside all the legal issues about perjury and depositions, the president has admitted to two morally wrong actions – first he committed adultery and second he lied to the American people when he said he "didn't have sex with that woman." The consequences of those two wrongs are enormous. Let's look at just a couple of examples.

Not counting the costs of the investigation, millions of dollars have been spent in every conceivable form of media and the world has had to deal with the consequences of what he has done. How much good could have been done with all that money and air time on almost any other topic? Mr. Clinton is the first person responsible for that waste of money and media attention. Others are also responsible but they could not have gotten involved if he hadn't committed adultery and lied in the first place.

Another consequence – parents have had to explain to their children what he did and the distinctions the president tried to make between various types of sex acts. He brought explicit sexual talk and language to the breakfast table and living rooms. He is responsible for that consequence.

He is also responsible for the examples he has given our youth, including sexual immorality, that doing anything you want is OK if you don't caught at it, and that lying to get out of a jam is a good idea. In doing so he has also squandered his opportunity to inspire to goodness.

One of the most important consequences of his actions has been his encouragement of the reaction of the American people that "it was only adultery" and "it was only a lie." He has chosen to lower the moral standards of our country.

The list of the consequences of his actions could go on and on. He is responsible for those consequences and until he begins to publicly do something about those consequences his words that he "takes full responsibility" for what he has done is just another lie.

Some people will say that holding him accountable for the consequences of his actions is not the Christian thing to do, instead we should forgive him and let the country go back to normal. I am totally in favor of forgiving him, but with true forgiveness, not the unreal pretending that something did not happen which we often use in place of real forgiveness.

Forgiveness is acceptance that a relationship has been damaged or destroyed and that pain and hurt have happened. Forgiveness remembers that pain and hurt and goes beyond it into healing. Forgiveness is not cheap, it is hard work, and includes accountability and responsibility on the part of the person doing the forgiving. Mr. Clinton has caused deep moral wounds in our country. Forgiving him must include the healing of those wounds which he can help do by accepting the consequences of his actions.

Mr. Clinton has done three moral wrongs and admitted to two. The first was adultery, the second was lying to the American people, and the third was pretending to take responsibility for these acts but not actually doing so. It is this third moral wrong that is probably the worst.

My foster son eventually learned to accept the consequences of his actions, but not before spending time in jail. The young drunk driver eventually learned to accept that it was the consequence of his decision to drink and drive that caused the death of his friend. It is my prayer, and the prayer of many parents and clergy who have to face the consequences of Mr. Clinton's three moral wrongs, that he accepts responsibility for the consequences of his actions as well.

September 26, 1998

What Makes An Action Right Or Wrong?

In the middle ages, troops of players traveled throughout Europe performing what we now call "morality plays." These were simple melodramas where good was rewarded and evil was punished. They were often used as a means to educate the common people about good and bad, sin and love, punishment and reward.

As we Americans [as well as the rest of the world] endure the national "morality play" being lived out in Washington, many of us are sick and tired of the subject of morality. But the lessons this play offers us are too valuable to ignore.

Many of the lessons of the Clinton/Lewinsky morality play center around the belief in America that there is nothing really "right" or "wrong." The argument for this says that if a person thinks it is right for him or her, then it is right. If a person thinks it is wrong, then it is wrong. Thus things like cheating, shoplifting, tax evasion, lying, sexual activity, adultery have no intrinsic right or wrong to them except what the person involved feels to be true. Some people carry this view to actions such as murder or sex with children.

One thing that can make a difference between whether a person thinks some action is right or wrong is "getting caught." Many people think an action they have done was right until they get caught. Then after the act is exposed they claim remorse and offer an apology. But often the remorse and apology are for getting caught rather than what they did in the first place.

Are some actions intrinsically right or wrong? Religious traditions have always thought so. But religions have done a very poor job in explaining why such actions are right or wrong. Most of the time good actions have been ignored and wrong actions have been given out as lists.. Thus we can find in the Bible or in religious books lists of sins. There is often no reason given for why such and such an action is a sin except that it listed under the list of sins.

For Bible based religions that is reason enough – if it is listed as a sin then it is a sin because the Bible says so. For religions that believe in the Bible but are not Bible based, such as my own, simply being listed in the biblical list of sins is not enough, but then my Church made the mistake in listing sins and saying they were wrong because the Church said they were wrong. In today's world most people believe that just because an action is listed in the Bible or in some Church catechism is not a good enough reason to believe that action is wrong. They want a reason why.

The "why" that makes an action right or wrong is the effect that action has on the person who does it, as well as on that person's relationships with other people. The best definition of sin is *self-destructive behavior*. Items on lists of sins are on the list because performing those actions causes destruction in the person who does the action. Sin as self-destructive behavior is a concept that is so foreign to most Americans, especially younger Americans, that it honestly makes no sense to them.

A good example of this is cheating. Recent studies tell us that the majority of high school and college students cheat on a regular basis. When asked if cheating is wrong the majority said it is wrong only if you get caught; if you get away with it then it is right. The fact that cheating hurts the person who cheats as well as everyone else is totally ignored.

Self-destructive behavior is anything that makes a person less good, less noble, less beautiful, less holy, less of a person. It is anything that makes a person's relationship with the rest of humanity less good, less noble, less beautiful, less holy, less of a relationship. Getting caught or exposed might be added pain, but the destruction has already happened when the sin was done. Monica Lewinsky did not damage herself when she got exposed, she did it when she made her choices with Mr. Clinton. All of Mr. Clinton's affairs and sexual adventures have been actions of self-destruction that have made him less than he was before.

Self-destruction is not true only if the person believes it to be true, it is true in and of itself. Actions take their effect from the context in which they happen, the intention of the person doing them, and the consequences that follow from them. The same action can sometimes be good and sometimes be sinful.

Thus sexual intercourse in the context of marriage is a source of God's grace, and sexual intercourse outside of marriage damages the people who do it. Telling the truth builds a person up, telling a lie tears a person down. Just as athletic training strengthens a person, moral training strengthens a person. Consistent sinful actions cause consistent destruction.

Spiritual, moral, and social maturity come to persons when they realizes that there are things they might wish they could do, such as steal something or have an affair, that they will not do because it will change and damage them on the inside. They won't do it because they might get caught, nor because the action is on some list, but because the action is intrinsically wrong.

Watching the incredible self-destruction that litters our national morality play, no one should underestimate the power of sin to destroy those who commit it.

October 31, 1998

What Do Christians Do When They Go To Church?

This is the third in my series of columns comparing the under-standings of the Catholic Church and the evangelical fundamentalist churches on a variety of issues. The first described the differences in the meaning of the Church and the second on the use of the Bible. This column is about the different views on what it means to worship God.

On all three of these issues the other Protestant Churches have their own teachings.

I choose to compare Catholics and evangelical fundamentalists because in this era in which some people are saying that all Christian denominations are the same, it is important to realize that there are major essential differences between the denominations. I compare Catholicism with evangelical fundamentalism because its beliefs of-ten stand in sharp contrast with Catholicism. But the same type of comparison can be made between any Churches or denominations by objectively and honestly comparing what is believed on a spe-cific topic, such as The Church, The Bible, or worship.

The most important difference between Catholicism and evan-gelical fundamentalism is in the understanding of how God relates to humankind.

Catholics believe God relates both individually and communally. Catholicism is a communal religion in which God's grace can be shared from person to person. Thus for Catholics the Church is the People of God, the Bride of Christ, and God has a relationship with the community of believers. Each baptized person has both a per-sonal and a communal relationship with God. Catholics believe God has given the Church an organizational structure including an or-dained clergy.

Evangelical fundamentalism believes God relates to humans in-dividually. Evangelical fundamentalism is an individualistic reli-gion in which God's grace must come directly to each person from

65

God. For evangelical fundamentalists each person who is saved has a personal relationship with God. When those individuals gather that is called Church. Since salvation is totally personal and individual, the Church is a help to accepting personal salvation but not part of it.

It is this difference in how God relates to humankind that marks all aspects of the differences between Catholicism and evangelical fundamentalism. When we apply this difference to worship the implications are very clear.

The evangelical writer Sally Morgenthaler says that worship is "an intentional response of praise, thanksgiving, and adoration to The God, the One revealed in the Word, made known and accessible to us in Jesus Christ and witnessed in our hearts through the Holy Spirit (truth)." This is done by a person through song, praise, prayer, and preaching.

When an individual goes to an evangelical fundamentalist church on a Sunday he or she expects to sing, to give praise, to pray, and to listen to the Word of God and a sermon on the Word of God. Other individuals will be there doing the same thing. These activities, organized differently in different places but containing the same basic elements, constitute thanksgiving, praise, and adoration of God because that is what those individuals intend by those actions.

Catholicism would agree with Morgenthaler's description but say it does not go far enough. For Catholics worship is more complicated and more difficult to define. There is personal worship called private prayer or devotions, and there is public communal worship called liturgy. In the Second Vatican Council the Catholic Church said that, "The liturgy is rightly seen as an exercise of the priestly office of Jesus Christ.. . . (using) signs perceptible by the senses." The Catholic Church also says that Liturgy, "makes the Church present and manifests her as the visible sign of the communion in Christ between God and men. It engages the faithful in the new life of the community and involves the conscious, active, and fruitful participation of everyone."

When a Catholic goes to Church on Sunday he or she expects to be bonded by Jesus Christ the High Priest with himself and with the other full members of the Church at the level of the soul. Led by Jesus through the ordained priest these bonded souls then communally offer a divine sacrifice to God. This sacrifice gives praise and thanksgiving to God. This is done by the proclamation of the Word and preaching, and by officially asking the Holy Spirit to enter into the bread and wine so that they become the body and blood of Jesus Christ, which in turn is received by the joined souls of the Church as "common union." All of these actions are accompanied by songs and prayers. Catholics call this the sacrifice of the Eucharist, the banquet of the Eucharist, the celebration of the Eucharist, the sacrament of the Eucharist – commonly called Mass.

Comparing these two totally different understandings of worship and different expectations, it is no wonder that members of one group find it difficult to be at the a worship service of the other. It is easier for Catholics to go as individuals to evangelical fundamentalist services because at least at the level of structure it is similar to the Liturgy of the Word of the Mass. It is often very difficult for evangelical fundamentalists to be comfortable at Catholic Mass, not just because of the vestments and ritual, but because they correctly perceive that because they are not full members of the Catholic Church they are not fully part of the bonded souls that are celebrating the Mass.

What we all must remember is that while the differences between these Churches in understanding how God relates to us and how God wants to be worshiped are extremely important, at the same time God loves all of us, and hears all of our prayers.

November 28, 1998

Choosing A Jesus To Suit Our Fancy

The Last Temptation of Christ, both the book by Nikos Kazantzakis and the movie by Martin Scorsese, were hailed by some as great Christian literature and denounced by other as blasphemy. The musicals *Jesus Christ Superstar* and *Godspell* had similar, if not quite so intense, reactions. No one has used the phrase great Christian literature to describe the modern play *Corpus Christi*, which depicts Jesus and the apostles as practicing homosexuals, in fact almost all Christians recognize it as blasphemy.

Writings about Jesus are controversial because most authors emphasize those aspects of the life of Jesus they like. Their critics immediately say they have deliberately distorted the truth. Kazantzakis, a great Greek author, was obsessed with the idea that Jesus struggled with being both God and man. The story of this struggle, *The Last Temptation of Christ* was for Kazanzakis an act of faith. But those whose image of Jesus does not contain that struggle are scandalized by even the thought that Jesus might consider abandoning his divine mission, choosing instead to be human, to marry, and to have children.

Most Christians who have delved deeply into Jesus have found themselves confronted by conflicting images. The God-man hero of the Gospels is incredibly complex. We often resolve the complexity by choosing those images which comfort and reassure us, ignoring or even rejecting those which we do not like. We tend to gather with people who share our image of Jesus and look askance at those who hold other ideas.

The six most common Jesus images are Jesus as teacher, Jesus as King, Jesus as Holy One, Jesus as brother, Jesus as liberator, and finally Jesus as questioner. [I am indebted to the theologian Richard McBrien for an explanation of some of these images.]

Jesus as teacher appeals to people who want and need answers, security, clarity. This is the Jesus who reveals God to us, tells us what to do, promises salvation to those who have ears to hear his message. At its best the image of Jesus as teacher inspires and enriches us; at its worse the image of Jesus as teacher has been used to justify inquisitions and heresy trials.

Jesus as King is also Jesus as judge. This is the strong, powerful, severe Jesus often seen in Byzantine art, or depicted as coming on clouds at the end of time. At its best it is the Lord of the world who will draw all things back to himself, whose reign will be without end. At its worst this image is the owner and custodian of a world increasingly sinful and in need of punishment, a world in which those who reject his clear teaching and moral instructions are going to be firmly sent to the fires of hell.

Jesus the Holy One is Jesus as God. It is the image of much Christian art and literature, the Jesus with the long hair, radiant robes, and heavenly gaze. It is the Jesus of Catholic statues and holy cards. At its best this is the Jesus of the transfiguration, the crucifixion, and the resurrection, the God who has chosen to save us. At its worst this is a Jesus remote and distant from humanity, unreal and often scary.

Jesus as brother is Jesus as human. This is the Jesus who goes around telling people he loves them and urging them to love one another. He cures, heals and forgives sins. At its best this is the warm loving Jesus who knows each person by name. At its worse this image of Jesus has no standards, allows everything, and becomes the ultimate 60's love child who invites everyone to the eternal end of the world party in heaven.

The image of Jesus as liberator is the friend of prostitutes and tax collectors, the critic of the social order who gives everything to the poor and bridles at hypocrisy and deceit. This Jesus denounced the pharisees, rejected the high priests, and defied Pilate by his silence. At its best this is Jesus who affirms the value and nobility of each and every human being, brings freedom by his grace, and gives his followers the courage to love the poor. At its worst this image of Jesus is used to put his followers above the law, approve the murder of abortionists, or condone racist militia groups.

The first five images of Jesus have a long history in Christian tradition. While the sixth image has existed from the days of the early Church it has become common only in modern times. The image of Jesus as questioner is Jesus as a growing changing human being, struggling with how to reconcile his divinity and humanity, how to be both God and man. At its best this is Jesus as model for humanity as we struggle to make sense out of the violence and destruction around us, as we try to deal with complex moral and social issues. At it worst this is Jesus as a confused self-absorbed anti-hero, mumbling in parables, uncertain of his purpose, making no absolute judgements about anything.

All too often we choose one or at most two of these images and reduce Jesus to only that, imprisoning ourselves in a distortion of who he really is. For the real Jesus is all of these and more. If we hope to have any real relationship with Jesus, we must accept and come to know him as he is, as complex and powerful as he is, as rich and varied as he is.

Those new little games and symbols with the initials WWJD, standing for "What Would Jesus Do?" are cute. But Jesus as King and Judge might do something very different from Jesus as liberator, or Jesus as brother. To be a real Christian we must resist the modern tendency to simplify Jesus. We must instead let him into our lives in all his marvelous complexity.

December 26, 1998

Religious Pluralism And Moral Pluralism

When I was a child, growing up in Boise, this was the Christmas season. It was a Christian time in America, a Christian season, a Christian country. At least that was how it seemed. Boise's very small Jewish community must have celebrated Hanukkah, but if so we never heard about it. Christmas was the only holiday in my childhood Decembers.

The world has changed. Now this is the "Holiday season." Neighbors celebrate not only Christmas and Hanukkah but also Kwanzaa, and this year Ramadan falls during December. We also have those among us who celebrate the Winter Solstice or give semi-religious meaning to the New Year.

All of this has changed because we have become multicultural. But is this change good or bad? Does a believer in Christ have any business acknowledging or becoming involved with a Jewish or Moslem feast, or the African American Kwanzaa or the New Age Winter Solstice? There is a major religious debate about these questions, a debate centered on the meanings of two words – *multicultural* and *tolerance*.

What is at the center of this debate is not simple religious pluralism, but the belief that American Christianity is being forced to accept and tolerate the sharing of religious holidays as the first step in a slippery slope leading to toleration of ethical and morals positions which violate traditional Christian values, such as multi-party sexual activity, abortion, homosexuality, witchcraft, polygamy, etc.

One point of view sees the new multiculturalism and the demand to be tolerant of it as truly dangerous to the collective faith and therefore dangerous to the country. This position sees America as first and foremost a Christian country, the most tolerant and benign of all Christian countries, but still a country founded on Christian [more specifically Protestant Christian] values.

The people who believe this way say that those who belong to

71

non-Christian religions and worship non-Christian Gods, or even no God at all, are free to do so. But it is Christians who allow them that freedom. Therefore they have the responsibility to let the historic and majority Christian faith have its right to be the civic religion of the nation.

These people believe there was once a Golden Age when America was Christian. There was a generic form of Protestant Christian prayer in public schools, at public gatherings, and in legislative chambers. Christmas was a holiday because it was Jesus' birthday, and Thanksgiving was a day to thank God for making America his favorite country.

This was the time of the melting pot, the time when anyone [especially if they were white] could come to America from any land, and once here begin the slow blending process of becoming American. Part of this assimilation was acceptance of the American civic religion, even by members of the two biggest non-Protestant religions, Catholics and Jews.

The people who want a return to this Golden Age believe this system produced red blooded American men and women who made this country great. It is precisely the loss of this Protestant Christian heart and soul of our land which has produced the moral, spiritual and ethical messes we must now endure. The acceptance of other religious holidays as equal to Christmas is just the first step down the slope of allowing multiculturalism to destroy all Christian values.

There is a second point of view which claims there never was a Golden Age, but rather a religious caste system which has now finally been toppled. The people who believe this way see the efforts of the first group to restore prayer in schools and "put Christ back into Christmas" as dangerous and illegal. These people speak a new language and advocate a new value – multiculturalism.

This new value says that Christians can celebrate Christmas, but equally important is the fact that Moslems can observe Ramadan, and the Jews can celebrate Hanukkah, and others can have Kwanzaa or Winter Solstice. They see multiculturalism as a form of religious freedom, with the values of each religion coexisting side by side.

These people say that Christianity's hold on American civic religion must be loosened and that American Christians must learn to live equally with all other religions. If that were the only issue the debate might be easy.

But there are those among this group who go further and say that there are values within Christianity which conflict with religious freedom, and that not only do the Christians have to tolerate religious pluralism, but Christians must become tolerant of ethical and moral positions which violate traditional Christian values. Christians must not be allowed to impose their moral positions on issues such as adultry, abortion, etc. on other people. Christians must be tolerant of moral pluralism.

My own Catholic Church [as well as many mainline Protestant churches] finds itself in both camps. Before Vatican II we had very little respect for other religions, we were religiously intolerant. We also share a nostalgia for the Golden Age of fifty or seventy five years ago when Christian values were publicly affirmed.

But we now have strong modern Church teachings from Vatican II and modern popes which are crystal clear in our obligation to revere and respect other religious traditions, and ensure that all people can have the freedom to pray according to their own beliefs. We also have teachings which tell us to encourage inculturation within our own Church and worship, and honor and believe in religious pluralism.

But when it comes to the second stage of multiculturalism, when we are asked to move from religious pluralism to moral pluralism, Catholicism cannot do so. It views moral pluralism as moral indifference.

It is this jump from saying that Kwanzaa or Ramadan can share equal holiday status with Christmas to saying that all moral and ethical positions are equally valid that is at the heart of the multicultural problem. One side says that unless Christianity, with its values, is restored as the civil religion, America will become a moral cesspool. The other side says that American Christians must not only tolerate religious pluralism but also moral pluralism.

What all Christians have to ask themselves is: when does tolerance become indifference, when does non-judgmental become just a lack of standards?

January 30, 1999

Looking Good By Manipulation And Deceit

Teachers and preachers of some religions teach things which are untrue about the beliefs and practices of other religions. As this special month of peace and healing sponsored by Interfaith Ministries of Central Oregon comes to a close, this is a good time to look at these deliberate distortions of the truth. I do this because real peace and healing can only come by exposing evil and promoting truth and light.

Good religious dialogue requires accurate and truthful presentation of the teachings and doctrines of various Churches, and a clear presentation of the differences between them. For example, the Catholic teaching on sacraments is different than the Presbyterian teaching, or the Mormon teaching, or the Episcopal teaching, but all these groups can understand and respect the differences.

But there are groups within Christianity who deliberately distort the doctrines and practices of other religions with the firm purpose of tearing down these other religions. In America the three religions which have suffered the most from having their doctrines and practices distorted are Catholics, Mormons, and Jews. I want to examine a few of the untruths told about each of those religions.

Untruth #1 – Catholics Worship Mary

A non-Catholic student in Redmond said that in her Church the pastor had taught them that Catholics worship Mary. The pastor said that Catholics are idolaters, pagan worshipers of images. He said that Catholics are not Christian.

The truth is that Catholics do not worship Mary. Catholics only worship God. They honor Mary and other saints, and pray to them because they are members of the family, members of the People of God. Catholics do not worship images or idols, and are certainly Christians.

74

A variation on this distortion comes in the form of books like the one written by a man in Bend (published in Eugene) which calls the Catholic Church the beast of the book of Revelation or the whore of Babylon. These are hate-filled books, crammed with literally hundreds of untrue statements.

Untruth #2 – The Jews Killed Jesus And Cannot Go To Heaven.

Young children in Bend are being taught that the Jews killed Jesus and that Jews cannot go to heaven. These children are being told to tell this to their young Jewish schoolmates. The little Jewish kids hear this and get scared and confused. This anti-Semitic accusation has been used for hundreds of years to justify bias and hatred against Jewish people.

The truth is that it is absolutely inaccurate to say that "The Jews" killed Jesus. The story of the death of Jesus in the four Gospels is a story of events in Jerusalem 2000 years ago. Jews and Romans were involved. Jesus and the apostles were Jews, the high priests and the crowd were Jews. Pilate and the soldiers were Romans. There were Jews on both sides. But the people responsible for the death of Jesus were the people who were there, at that time, in that place – some were Jewish, some were Romans. Jewish people who were not there had no responsibility for what happened, any more than Roman people who were not there had responsibility for what happened.

Untruth #3 – Catholics Think The Pope Is Always Infallible

A Bend religious counselor told someone recently that Catholics are such stupid people that they believe the pope is personally infallible, that he can never make a mistake. Anyone who has seriously studied any theology knows that the Catholic teaching on infallibility has nothing to do with the pope being personally infallible. This counselor chose to tell this person something which was untrue just to make the Catholic Church look silly.

The truth is that the Catholic teaching on infallibility is a very specific and specialized teaching. Simply put it says that when the Church, speaking through the pope, after consultation with the bishops of the world, clarifies a matter of faith or morals consistently taught in the Church for 2000 years, the Holy Spirit will guide the Church to be correct. This has only happened twice in the past 400 years.

75

Catholics believe the pope is to be paid attention to when he teaches anything, but on personal issues he is as likely to make mistakes as anyone else. It rains when he says it is going to be sunny, and Poland loses soccer games even when the pope says they are going to win. The pope is a human being like anyone else.

Untruth #4 – Mormons Are Not Christians

Some religions in the western United States target Mormons, and one of the favorite untruths to spread is that Mormons are not Christians. The Church of Jesus Christ of Later Day Saints (the official title of the Church commonly called the Mormons) is said to be a cult, filled with evil people, dedicated to destroying true Christianity.

The truth is that the Mormons have a different understanding of who God is and how God works from most of the rest of the Christian religions. Because of this they have a different understanding of who Jesus is and how Jesus is related to God. But just because they define the words differently does not mean they are not Christians. Mormons are Christians because they want to call themselves Christians. They have as much right to understand Jesus in their way as other Christians have to understand Jesus in the way they do.

The list of these religious untruths could go on and on. I thought very seriously about calling these distortions "lies" but in the end decided not to because the word "lie" indicates deliberate misinformation and sometimes these religious teachers may just be ignorant of the truth. The Redmond pastor may actually believe that Catholics worship Mary, or the Bend counselor may really believe that Catholics think the pope is personally infallible, or some people may be convinced that Mormons are not Christians — but just being ignorant of the truth does not give a person the freedom to teach untruths. Teaching anti-Semitic hatred to children is a special form of distortion, a real lie which has caused the deaths of six million people in this century alone.

One of the tests that every church-going person should use to evaluate the church he or she attends is this: If the preacher or teacher has to denounce another religion or faith to make their own look good, that is not a Church where God is found.

February 27, 1999

Inventory For Churchgoers And Non-churchgoers

From the earliest years of the Church the forty days before Easter have been a period of reflection, repentance, and renewal. This has come to be called Lent, from a word meaning springtime.

During these days people are asked to give time to self-reflection and self-examination, to do spiritual spring cleaning, to do a spiritual inventory. In modern times when life has become so hectic, this time for oneself is even more important than in a simpler age. This is true not only for the people who go to church, but especially for the people who choose not to do so.

The decision to be involved or not be involved in spirituality is a major decision, and one which should be seriously made, not just one which happens by chance. It also should be rethought and renewed at least once a year.

But how does a person do a spiritual inventory? What does it mean to do spiritual spring cleaning?

What follows is a list of questions. I find them disturbing, and sometimes difficult to answer. But they make me think, and constantly reevaluate the state of my own soul. I need that.

It is best if the answers are written down. Some are to be answered by one's self, some are to be answered together with family members. This is not easy because cleaning is never easy. But the results – a clean heart and soul – are worth the effort.

Section One
Personal Questions

1) If God were asked to describe me, what would he say?

2) What does God see as my greatest strength? What does God see as my greatest weakness?

3) Where does my image of myself differ from God's image of me?

4) What does it mean to communicate with God? How do I communicate with God?

5) What is the most wonderful and best thing I have ever done for myself? What is the most wonderful and best thing I have ever done for others?

6) What does it mean to me to do something wrong? What is my favorite wrong thing to do?

7) What do I understand to be the meaning of forgiveness? Does forgiveness mean something different if I am the one forgiving or if I am the one being forgiven?

8) If I were asked, "What is your spiritual existence?" or "How is your spiritual life?" How would I answer?

9) What is the role of other people in my spiritual life? What is the role of those close to me? What is the role of those at a distance?

10) What responsibility do I carry for the spiritual lives, the holiness, of my wife or husband, parent or child, neighbor or friend?

Section Two
Questions To Be Answered Together With Family Members
[Family members means primarily husbands and wives. It can mean older children or other adults who are close confidants.]

11) How would each member of the family describe the personal spiritual life of each of the other members of the family?

12) Name one specific event which each individual member of the family has done to build up the spiritual life of the other members?

13) Give an example of each family member sharing God with another family member.

14) What would be an action which each family member could stop doing which would help all the other family members?

15) Is the spiritual life of each family member the concern of the others? Should it be?

16) Does this family communicate with God? How? Does that communication include listening to God? How does God speak to this family?

17) What responsibility does a husband have for his wife's spiritual life? What responsibility does a wife have for her husband's spiritual life? What responsibility do children have for their parent's spiritual lives?

18) What is the family sin of this family? Has the sin changed over the years? Who is the custodian of the family sin?

19) On a scale of one to ten, if ten is the perfect family, where does each family member think this family is and why?

20) How would each member of the family evaluate his or her own spiritual life and the lives of the family members using as a criterion the phrase "Good religion is good mental health?"

21) If God were asked to describe this family, what would he say? Why?

If you have found this list of questions interesting and challenging, that is great. But if you have read through this list and thought to yourself: "There is no way I will ask those questions of myself, and there is no way I am going to discuss these things with my husband, wife, parents, or children," that refusal to even ask the questions says your spiritual life is not healthy.

If you will not answer the questions and you are presently a church going person, you need to really think about what you are getting from church. If you are not a church going person and will not even consider evaluating your spiritual life, that means something is seriously wrong.

This is not an easy exercise for anyone, but it is beneficial. Good luck and Happy Lent!

March 27, 1999

The Most Godlike Thing A Person Can Do

If Jesus came to earth, if Jesus came back and reappeared among us, would we know it? Would we recognize him? What would he do to let us know it's Jesus? Or, to put the question another way, if one of us wanted to act like Jesus, what would he or she do? What is the most Godlike action a human being can perform?

The possibilities are endless – curing cancer or AIDS or heart disease, eliminating poverty, bringing peace to the world, ending political corruption. But Jesus didn't do any of those things when he was here before, he gave us the values and example so we could do those ourselves. No, I think Jesus would do again the one action which was his most Godlike, and the one action a person can do to be the most like God. He washed feet.

Nowhere in the New Testament does Jesus show himself to be God more than in that famous moment in the thirteenth chapter of John's Gospel where he bends over and washes the feet of his friends. They don't have a clue about what he is doing. He knows that, but he washes their feet anyway. Jesus is showing us how God acts in the presence of human beings – he bends over and washes their feet. The God who created the universe, who can control everything, who knows all that is to be known, bends over and washes their feet.

Why does he do it? Why is that such a Godlike thing to do? Jesus says he does it because he is the teacher and Lord, and washing feet is what teachers and Lords do. He says he does it to give us an example of how to treat one another. He does it because it is the perfect act to symbolize how truly powerful God is.

All the wisdom and power and might of God is not for control or intimidation. God is not powerful so he can rule over us. God is powerful so he can love us, and allow us to love him. He serves us because it is in service that true love is manifested. And God does not just love, God is love. When pure love becomes alive, when pure love taken a human body, it shows itself to be pure love by washing feet.

But Jesus is giving us a tough example to follow. There is something about washing feet that is not appealing. If I want to act like God, I want to act like God when he is doing something else, like destroying the Assyrians or healing the man born blind. That's just feels a lot better than washing feet. But Jesus didn't tell us that we were to imitate his example by doing fun things like walking on water, he said we were to imitate his example by doing powerful things like washing feet. That is how we are to show our love and reverence for one another.

Now we realize that Jesus is speaking more than just literally, and that we do not have to actually wash feet to imitate him. We can do that by performing many different types of important service.

There is however a strong tendency to keep moving away from the literal washing of feet and never actually do that specific action. So once a year we as Church set before ourselves the celebration of the washing of feet. It takes place at the Holy Thursday Service, the Mass of the Lord's Supper. It is an incredibly powerful liturgical ritual.

There are a couple of ways it can be done. In small churches the priest removes some of his vestments and gets down on the floor and pours water and wipes the feet of six or twelve men and women. [If the priest is infirm, then someone else takes his place.]

In larger churches with lots of room there is another very meaningful way in which the washing can be done. The priest washes the feet of a few people who then go and get buckets and set up other washing stations in other places. Sometimes there are eight or ten places. Anyone who wants to have his or her feet washed can do so, and anyone who wants to wash feet can take the place of a person who has been washing for awhile. The washing goes on as long as people want it to, then Mass continues.

It is difficult to describe either the feeling of having your foot washed or washing the foot of someone else. Like all non-verbal liturgical prayer it is beyond emotion and is centered deep in the soul. Both actions are humbling and ennobling at the same time. There is a true feeling of doing an action of God when you wash someone's feet, and truly a feeling of being loved by God when someone washes your feet in God's name. Many people in the middle ages thought that the washing of feet was a sacrament and having done it, I can see why they could believe that.

The Pope always kisses the feet he washes. I am ashamed to admit I have never been able to do that. Hopefully I will someday be holy enough to do so.

Many churches besides the Catholic ones have the liturgical ritual of the washing of feet on Holy Thursday. If you are a member of a church which does it, make every effort to be there and participate. If your church does not wash feet, you might suggest that they begin to do so.

If you really want to act like God – go, wash feet.

April 24, 1999

Thank God For Rocky Johnson

"Rocky Johnson" – it's not a name that inspires confidence. If names can evoke images, my image of a person named Rocky Johnson would be a big burly longshoreman or lumberjack. I see him getting into fights fairly easily, making promises he doesn't always keep, doing stupid things then regretting them later. A good man, but not a leader, someone not really very dependable.

Then I realize that if we used modern naming methods the person who dominates the early Christian Church, its leader, the person God himself selected for the post would be called Rocky Johnson. In the 16th chapter of St. Matthew's Gospel Jesus says, "Blessed are you, Simon, son of John . . . I call you Rock (Peter)." Or said another way, "Simon Johnson, from now on I am calling you Rocky."

Calling St. Peter by the name Rocky Johnson helps give me a much greater understanding of the humanity and "realness" of him. When we preface someone's name with the title saint, and give them only a first name, that person moves out of the world of regular people into sort of a superhuman realm.

But Rocky belongs in the real world, he was very much a real person. If the rest of the apostles were teenagers, which is very possible, then Rocky was one of the older ones. He was married, although we know nothing of his wife. He had been a fisherman when Jesus invited him to become a disciple and eventually an apostle.

Rocky is almost a comic figure, always blurting out something (as at the Transfiguration) or doing something rash (his attempt to walk on water) or making shallow promises ("I will never deny you"). There is a little cowardly lion or Homer Simpson quality to him.

But he is so sincere, he tries so hard that he becomes lovable. After Pentecost, he gets his courage. Rocky is the dominant figure of the early Church, he is the main figure, the main man. This one-time coward now speaks out with clarity and conviction. Luke's account of Rocky's speeches in the Acts of the Apostles gives the impression that there may have been some generous editing, but the power behind his words is evident. We know he did not personally write the letters that carry his name, but it is impressive that the real author chose to use Peter's name to give the letters stature.

Another fascinating person from our family is Mary from the town of Magdala. She is the other great figure of the earliest days of the Church before Paul begins his rise to prominence.

We today have a hard time understanding that Mary Magdalene was incredibly important in the earliest Church, much more important than Mary the mother of Jesus. She was revered and esteemed, imitated and admired.

What cost her fame was that a misguided pope in 499 confused this Mary with Mary the sister of Martha and with the unnamed prostitute who washed Jesus's feet. He combined all three into one person and ever since there has been this legend that Mary Magdalene was the great sinner who reformed when she met Jesus. They were three separate women but Mary Magdalene's reputation has suffered for 1500 years because of it.

Mary's importance came because she was the first witness to the Resurrection, as well as a witness to the crucifixion. While the men disciples were hiding under the bed in fear, the women followers of Jesus, led by Mary of Magdala, were both at the cross and out early Sunday morning to anoint the body. She became the "Apostle of Truth" and the "Apostle to the Apostles." In a culture where the testimony of a woman did not count, the importance the Gospels give to Jesus' decision to first appear to a woman and then give her the task of telling men, say much about the vital role of women in the earliest Church.

Mary of Magdala was also the person who supported the ministry of Jesus even before his death. Extra biblical writings tell us that she continued to play a very important part in the Church long afterward.

There is a wonderful legend that Mary was so upset with Pontius Pilate for allowing Jesus to die that she went to Rome to personally complain to the emperor. When her turn finally came to present him with a gift in thanks for seeing her, the gift was a red egg. She told the emperor that the egg was because her Jesus rose from the dead like new birth out of the egg. But the egg was red because Pilate caused Jesus to suffer and bleed. The emperor then transferred Pilate from Judea back to Rome for punishment. And that is one explanation for the origins of colored Easter eggs.

Rocky Johnson and Mary are saints, persons who have died and are now living with God, still involved with and influencing our lives. Saint Rocky and St. Mary have a great deal to teach us and model for us. Perfect people don't make good saints, imperfect people who try their best do. That is one of the reason why my Church is so conscious of the deceased heros and heroines from the past. They are both great role models and are also gracing us with the continued presence as guides and inspirations.

What is so valuable about them and all the saints is that they are real, they are family, and they belong to us.

May 29, 1999

Who Will God Let Into Heaven? (Part One)

A man died, went to heaven and met Saint Peter. They began to walk through heaven with Peter explaining all the places and things the man was seeing. As they passed the doors to one big room St. Peter motioned to the man to be very quiet and they tiptoed past, then resumed regular conversation.

"What was that all about, tiptoeing and being so quiet?" the man asked.

"Oh, that's where the Catholics are. They think they're the only ones here."

That 1950's joke was a fairly accurate description of what my Church's views were then about who could make it into heaven. Then in the 1960's my church went through the experience of the Second Council of the Vatican and two of the major issues the council fathers faced were: 1) could non-Catholics go to heaven, and 2) could non-Christians go to heaven.

They did not ask the questions in exactly that way, and the path they traveled took three years and much heated discussion. It was very difficult for the Catholic Church, after 2000 years of existence, to face head on the reality that a great deal of the lack of unity among Christians was caused by the sinfulness of Catholic leaders in the past. It was also difficult to face the issues of all those religions which do not view Jesus Christ as the Son of God and Savior. The Council ended up issuing three documents on ecumenism, non-Christian religions, and religious freedom, and all three broke new ground.

The council fathers concluded that for all Christians God is present in the sacrament of baptism and found in each "ecclesial body" or church. Beyond that, God works with and within all sincere religious bodies, and that he does not restrict his love and salvation to just those who know him by his Christian name.

Popular Catholic culture had believed for so long that only Catholics could go to heaven that it was hard for many Catholic people to move beyond those beliefs. Many people asked the same questions some of the bishops had asked at the council, "If people from any religion can go to heaven, then why be a Catholic?" and "Does this mean all religions are equal and equally true?"

They are valid questions, and the answers, like most really good answers, are complicated. But they essentially end up saying that [from the Catholic understanding]: 1) all religions are not equally true, but God can be found in all of them; 2) some religions have a great deal more truth in them than others; 3) someone sincerely faithful to a religion or Church with less truth is still much closer to God than someone who is an indifferent member of one with more truth; and 4) God always rewards effort more than success.

What that means is that a good Buddhist or Jew or Moslem is much more likely to be close to God than a mediocre Catholic Christian or a mediocre Christian of any type. It means that having a relationship with God does not depend upon knowing God only under the name Jesus Christ. And it means that we who are Catholic Christians have to do a much better job of explaining just what being a Catholic means. We Catholics and all Christians can no longer just preach that all people must join us or they will go to hell.

But this teaching means much more than that, and has repercussions far beyond Catholicism. It does away with what had been the justification for religious persecution, religious discrimination, religious hatred. Freedom for and respect for other religious traditions is the foundation for a world free of the hatreds which killed 6 million Jews, one million Armenians, and countless other millions this century alone. Unfortunately ethnic and religious wars continue as we approach a new century, with Kosovo joining Ireland, Israel, the Sudan, and other places where people are killed in the name of the God they worship.

The first step in religious hatred and persecution is the condemnation of people's right to believe what they believe. And there are, even in our midst, still religions and denominations which teach that they alone are right and all others are to be condemned as wrong. Just a few years ago in Idaho I was publically condemned by a "Christian" pastor and told that because I was a Catholic I would "spend eternity in hell." I would be there with all the Jews, Hindus, Buddhists, Mormons, Episcopalians, Moslems, and all the rest who did not agree with his understanding of God, which he claimed to find in the New Testament of the Christian Bible.

I do not believe in, and my Church does not believe in, a God who will limit eternal salvation to those who only know him by one name, in one way, by one book, even a divinely inspired one. I do not believe in a God who would condemn 99% of the human race to eternal punishment. [Such a God must be an extremely poor designer of humanity if so many of his creations failed the test of life and ended up in hell.] I believe that when we arrive in heaven, and I believe the vast majority of us will, we will find people from every language, religion, and way of life.

When the Catholic Church redid all of our prayers for the Mass after Vatican II, they added a line in most Eucharist Prayers, the most major and important prayer in the Church. It is at the place where we pray for those who are with God in heaven, and it says: ". . . . for all who seek you with a sincere heart."

Who will be in heaven? Those who seek God with a sincere heart. They will find him. It is really that simple.

June 26, 1999

Who Will God Let Into Heaven? (Part Two)

I have been asked to comment further on my column last month about the teachings of my Church on who can share in eternal salvation in heaven. I stated that the Catholic Church struggled during the Second Vatican Council to come to terms with how non-Catholics and even non-Christians can be granted eternal life. The council teaches us that God does not restrict his love and salvation to those who know him by his Christian name.

One of the best ways to understand religious teaching is to study an example. Imagine a young boy in Kosovo whose soul was sent by God to be born into a good practicing Moslem family, and given the name Abdul. At age ten the only Christians he knows are the Serbian soldiers [Serbian Orthodox Christians] who first burn his home, then kill his parents and himself. The question is: Because ten year old Abdul was not a baptised Christian who professed Jesus as his Lord and Savior, does he automatically go to hell? Or further, do his parents automatically go to hell?

The issue must be put into terms of whether or not God is *limited* in what he can do for humanity. Is God limited in his love and salvation only to those people who know him in one way or by one name?

On the one hand are Christians who believe that the good and loving God who fills the Christian Bible and is found in every part of Christian history and tradition is found and best worshiped as Jesus the Christ. But, God is not limited to loving and giving salvation only to the people who call him by that name. These Christians cite the totality of the Bible and two thousand years of Christian tradition and teachings as their source for their belief.

On the other hand are Christians who say that God is indeed limited to loving and giving salvation only to those who call him by the name of Jesus the Christ. They cite specific lines of the New Testament of the Bible as the source for their belief.

I believe [and my Church teaches] that union with God comes

from an action of God to which we respond. God loves each and every person he has created. He does not hate any of us nor had he created us with the intention of sending us to eternal punishment. But not all people know him by the name of Jesus Christ, not all people know the Christian traditions, the liturgy, Bible, or sacraments. Those who seek God – no matter from where they start – with a sincere heart, will find God. But they have to seek and they have to be sincere.

Now it is important to realize that the God they will find is the real and only true God. This is the God of the Father, the Son, and the Holy Spirit. This is God who created all human beings (including Abdul). This is God who as God the Son became incarnate and became Jesus Christ. This is God who died on the cross and rose again. This is God who saved us. But . . . . . while it is that same God the sincere seeker will find, he or she might not find God under the name of Jesus Christ. It will be Jesus Christ who is found, but God does not limit himself to just the names we use for him.

The controversy over who is saved is centered on the issue of the "limitation" of God. Christianity has for almost two thousand years struggled with those who attempt to limit God to being and acting just as they wanted him to. In my Roman Catholic tradition this took the form of those who said that unless someone was a baptized practicing member of the Catholic Church, and observed all of the rules and regulations of the Church, then even God could not help him. There were people trying to preach this as late as the 1940s in Boston.

In other Christian bodies this limitation of God has taken the form of claiming that particular individual lines of the Bible, taken out of context, say that God can only be found in one specific way. He can only have a relationship with specific people who know him by one name and profess that name in a particular manner.

This need to limit God comes from a need for security and stability. Those Catholics of old who held so firmly to the belief that there was "no salvation outside the Church" wanted a Church with clear, hard and fast rules. They did not want to be challenged to think, to figure things out, to understand. No! They wanted simply to be told with absolute clarity what they had to do to get to heaven. When the inevitable rebellion came to overthrow this stifling form of paternalism in the Vatican Council, these security seekers had a difficult time.

Many of them and/or their children left the Catholic Church and found security by joining new and growing groups of people who had a new set of clear rules and regulations, based on limiting God to a few lines of the Bible. But the end result was the same, a security that came from knowing that following the rules meant going to heaven. And then some of these people went an important step further, saying that not following these specific rules meant going to hell.

There is no difficulty with the first step. That step says that if a person accepts salvation from God and shows this acceptance by doing specific things, then that person will be with God and will be saved. These specific things for Catholics are baptism into the Church, Mass, sacraments, etc.. For some other Christians these specific things are being born again and professing Christ as Lord and Savior. It is the second step, saying what happens to people who do not do show their acceptance of God's salvation by doing the specified things, where the difficulty arises.

For those (Catholics as well as other Christians) whose religious convictions are based on the overwhelming need for clarity and security, God *must* be limited to what they can understand. Somehow saying that there could be one set of rules for some people and at the same time people could get to heaven without following those rules is beyond understanding. At that point it becomes so easy to say that those who do not follow the specific rules go to hell.

But making that conclusion limits God's freedom to share his love as he wishes. My Church had a hard time coming to terms with that truth, but finally has done so.

I cannot limit God to my understanding of him. I know and believe Jesus Christ and profess him as my savior and the savior of all humankind. But if God wants to also save other people in other ways, I am not prepared to tell him he cannot do so.

The question which must be asked and answered by each priest, pastor, and Christian is the one which started this column: Because ten year old Abdul was not a baptised Christian who professed Jesus as his Lord and Savior, does he automatically go to hell?

July 31, 1999

Young Men And Women Today Are Not Stupid

Recent news reports tell us what we already knew – many young people today are reluctant to get married. These young men and women are not stupid. This highly educated segment of our society have concluded that marriage is not worth doing.

They have a fear of divorce and all the pain, suffering, and financial difficulties divorce brings. Many of them are products of divorce. They often see marriage and divorce as two sides of the same coin, quoting the old adage, "The main cause for divorce is marriage." Therefore many of them choose to live together without marriage. This is not just for the sex, but for financial and companionship reasons as well.

Some people condemn the young for their suspicion and rejection of marriage. They should not be condemned, in fact it is to their credit that they have looked at what many marriages have become in today's America – unhappy, torturous and doomed to end in divorce – and concluded that what our society calls marriage sucks.

Yet even the most cynical will admit that there are marriages that do last, and even more importantly there are marriages that flourish and are truly happy.

Why do some marriages flourish and others fail? Is getting married worth the risk? Why not just live together? The answers to these questions depend on what marriage actually is.

Marriage in our society has slowly drifted into two very different forms of relationships, one based merely on an **agreement** and one based on **consent**. An agreement is simply a decision between two people. Consent is both an agreement and much more, a gut level commitment between two people to give themselves body and soul to each other. In an agreement marriage the people don't really have to keep the vows they make, in a consent marriage they intend to keep them no matter what.

Both kinds of marriage have a civil contract and are recognized by the state. A divorce is the termination of the civil contract. But a civil contract is rarely enough to keep two people together. What is needed to keep them together is some type of spiritual bond. Since God intended that they not only stay together but be constantly growing in love, he created such a spiritual bond. This bond happens only when two people consciously intend to consent to each other. The spiritual bond comes from God by the consent of the couple, not by whether the wedding is in a religious setting.

There are two main kinds of agreement marriages – crippled marriages and designer marriages. There is one kind of consent marriage – a real marriage. What young people have come to think of as marriages are usually these crippled and designer marriages. Many have never seen a real marriage, where the people have consented and have a spiritual bond.

In a crippled marriage one or both parties are incapable of making consent, so all they have is an agreement. The cause of this incapacity might be immaturity, substance abuse, a victim of sexual abuse, or any of a host of other difficulties. These make a person able to mouth the words of consent and even intend them, but be totally unable to carry them out.

Designer marriages are more common and more dangerous than crippled marriages. In these either the man or woman or both deliberately leave some of the traditional parts of a real marriage consent out of the agreement. Because of the omissions there can be no consent, making a spiritual bond impossible.

Designer marriages usually come in four distinctive styles:

1) Leaving out commitment: A belief that "if it doesn't work out we can always get divorced" is the most common designer marriages omission. There is no commitment.

2) Leaving out faithfulness: There are people who get married but are open to the possibility of more than one sexual partner. If either partner to a marriage does not intend absolute faithfulness there is no bond which can hold them together.

3) Leaving out life-giving: Sexual intercourse is an essential part of marriage. In Christian theology, engaging in marital sexual intercourse is a source of God's grace and should be "life-giving" for the couple themselves and (especially in Catholic theology) open to the life-giving possibility of children.

4) Leaving out the happiness of the other party: Some people marry for what he or she can get out of the marriage. The person thinks, "It is my wife's or husband's job to make me happy, not my job to make him or her happy." These are marriages with incredible amounts of psychological and physical abuse. Marriages with abuse can never last.

Marriages based on mere agreement usually become unhappy. Even if there is no divorce the people are miserable.

But there are real marriages. These are based on consent. The two people involved have worked hard to get to know each other, they have similar values, beliefs, and lifestyles. Good and solid marriage preparation is an important part of getting people ready and able to give consent. At the wedding they actually mean the vows they make, they make a gut level commitment to give themselves body and soul to each other. After the wedding the work of making the marriage grow and deepen continues.

Joy, happiness and fulfillment are true and powerful advantages of a real marriage. These come from the need deep inside the human person to consent and commit one's self to another. To know and feel unconditional love. To be truly happy. To know that there will be someone there for richer or for poorer, in sickness and in health, for as long as both people live. To have God himself be the origin of the bond which holds two people together.

But are there any advantages of an agreement marriage over living together? I doubt it. I do not approve of living together, but it is often a much better choice than entering a crippled or designer marriage. The great difficult is that the exact characteristics which lead people to live together are those which create marriages of mere agreement. The vast majority of marriages of couples who first lived together do end up in divorce.

There is an instinct for survival and decency which keeps young people from entering into fatally flawed marriages. Some of them do not even know that there is the alternative of a real marriage. Some of them have never seen a real marriage, or know how to enter into a real marriage. So they live together.

But a change is slowly happening. Many young people today are coming to believe that anything worth doing is worth doing well. Our society must let that conviction become the jumping off point to help young people learn what consent, commitment, intention, vows, and a real marriage actually are. If young people today could see happy joyful people in real marriages they would imitate them. Young people today are not stupid.

August 28, 1999

The Role Of Religion In Promoting Hate

Bad religion promotes hate. Just like everything else in life, religion comes as good, bad, and in between. Good religion builds good mental health. Bad religion caters to mental instability, encourages dysfunction, and most serious of all, promotes hate.

Much of our culture is filled with hate and indifference. Hate is an emotion of gut level distain. Indifference is even worse – the total lack of care or concern. Hate makes us do something to hurt others, indifference allows us to do nothing to help others.

Hate is what makes people do things like the terrible shooting at the Jewish Community Center in California, the murder of the abortion doctor in New York, the dragging death of the black man in Texas, or the slaying of the gay student in Wyoming. We have a new category of crime in some states called "hate crimes" which recognize that there are some wrong deeds which are not just ordinarily wrong but are especially wrong.

Indifference is closely connected to hate, but is one step further down the ladder toward total evil. Indifference usually manifests itself when we know of someone else's hate and just let it happen. Indifference is not doing anything when something cries out to be done. Indifference is the silent accomplice, the enabler of hate.

Let me give an example of how hatred and indifference work together. A woman believes that abortion is wrong, and comes to the conclusion (often with the urging of some religious preacher) that abortion providers are murderers. She convinces herself that God has called her to end the life of the abortion provider. The people around her do nothing to stop her, nothing to move her away from her hatred. They have become her accomplices in the murder. Hate filled people are made possible by indifferent people.

Religion has played a major role in encouraging hatred and indifference. When a preacher advocates the hatred of any person, he or she becomes responsible for all hatred. I don't mean just the fringe churches such as Aryan Nations which openly preach hate. More dangerous are the established religions and their preachers who do not make a distinction between beliefs and the people who hold those beliefs.

Religions are free to teach that certain behaviors are wrong, such as abortion, capital punishment, homosexuality, physician assisted suicide. But when a religion or a preacher condemns not only the behavior but also people who advocate the behavior, that religion has turned bad and that preacher is teaching hate.

Hate fostered by religion often manifests itself in anti-Semitism and racism. There is a terrible history in Christianity of preaching and teaching hatred against Jews. This should be a closed chapter of Christian history, but it is not, as the holocaust and the recent L. A. shooting show. Churches, and there are said to be such churches in Central Oregon, which teach that modern day Jews are responsible for the death of Jesus Christ, are teaching hate. People who sit quietly in the pew while such hate is being preached are sinfully indifferent.

There are churches which teach hatred of homosexuals. My church and many other Christian denominations continue to struggle with the relationship between homosexuality and Christian morality. No one even knows for sure what homosexuality is. But some pastors thunder against it as if they did know, talking not just about homosexual activities but condemning gay men and lesbian women. That is teaching hate, and if people who listen to that sermon go out and commit crimes against gays, the preacher is responsible.

Standing in the pulpit and preaching is an awesome responsibility, especially in the area of moral theology and ethics. As someone who does it I must be very careful. I have to be able to accurately explain my church's teachings, advocating some actions and condemning other actions. But I can never condemn people.

For example, capital punishment and abortion are legal in this country. I believe and my church believes that those actions are morally wrong. I can teach that those actions are wrong, but I cannot stand in the pulpit and condemn the people who pull the switch or abort a child. I cannot teach hatred of anyone or any group, no matter who they are or anything they have done. I cannot teach hatred even of hate groups.

I also must teach that indifference about hatred is as bad as hatred. Yet I also must teach that we cannot be indifferent about moral evils such as abortion. We have to learn to be tolerant of differences without becoming indifferent to those differences.

I have mentioned a lot of distinct issues in this column from ethnic origins to moral behavior. I put them together because they are intimately connected in two important ways.

The first is that when a preacher teaches hate of any person, he or she opens the gate for all hate. If hating an abortion provider is morally justifiable then so is hating a Jew. If hating gays is preached from a pulpit, hating anyone is preached from that pulpit. Any hate justifies all hate.

The second thing which unites these various issues is that these are the issues which divide us, either by race, belief, or life style. We have to learn to live with people who not only disagree with us, but who may well be totally opposite of us. We have to become a mature enough society to know what we believe, be able to discuss and even debate with those who disagree, and never become disagreeable.

We who are Christian pastors must never misuse our pulpits to teach hate, condemn people, or tolerate indifference. We who are Christians must call our pastors to account if they misrepresent Jesus Christ to justify hatred, bias, and prejudice. We, Christians and all others, must actively work against racism, condemning white supremacy in all its forms as stupid, silly, and always wrong. But we also have to learn to live side by side with the racist, with the bigot, with the homophobe, with the anti-Semite, with the person who is pro-choice, pro-life, pro-death penalty, pro-whatever, even pro-hate.

Bad religion is responsible for promoting hatred, it is the responsibility of good religion to end it.

September 25, 1999

The Story Of Two Puppies

I was on retreat at a small retreat house on an estuary by the ocean. Marvelous woods separate the main complex from the water. The trees end at a cliff overlooking a small beach.

At the top of the cliff was a downed tree with a branch level to the ground. The smooth sheen on the top of the wood made it obvious that I was not the first person to find this natural bench, nor the first to sit there and watch the waves and attempt to pray.

It was with delight that I found my meditation interrupted by the sight of a puppy emerging from the brush below me and making his cautious way out onto the beach. He was soft brown in color with spots of white. He was little and very cute.

He approached the moving waves carefully, barking loudly to warn them that they had met their match. As a particularly large wave retreated he ventured forward, seemingly confident that the water's movement was a direct result of his command. When the next wave rushed forward he hesitated too long before turning to run. Carried back inland by the water he finally managed to get his footing, vainly trying to shake the foam from his coat.

For him it soon became a contest. He would rush the retreating water and then turn to escape the next wave. He must have kept at it for at least twenty minutes. I found myself being entertained and thanked God for the simplicity of the moment.

I had not noticed that at one end of the beach the retreat house property terminated at a wire fence until a boy appeared inside that fence. He was as fascinated by the puppy as I was, but he kept glancing back behind him.

Finally picking up a large stick he jumped the fence and ran to the puppy. They eyed each other and he extended his free hand, the puppy came forward and sniffed. The stick in his other hand gave me doubt until the boy picked up the soggy puppy and gave him a hug.

The boy, who appeared about seven or eight years old, put the stick gently in the puppy's mouth and then withdrew it, throwing it just a few feet away. The puppy caught onto the game at once and jumped from the boy's grasp to follow the stick.

But he was not about to bring it back. Once he had it in his teeth he looked at the boy and then turned and ran, making sure that the boy was behind him. They raced over the small beach in and out of the water until the boy finally caught up to the puppy and took the stick; only to throw it once more.

Again and again they threw and collected the stick, a boy and a dog, two puppies at play. I must have watched for over half an hour knowing I was in danger of missing the next conference but some-how justifying that this was really a better religious experience than one more talk would be.

Part of the mystique of the moment was that waves and cliff meant that I could not hear them, only an occasional bark would reach my ears. It was like a silent movie.

Suddenly I saw a man moving through the fence from which the boy had come.   Neither of them saw or heard him coming until he was upon them.

In one moment he had grabbed the boy by the hair with one hand and the stick with the other. As he raised it I called out but they could not hear me. The stick came down on the boy once, then again, then again and again and again. The boy tried to dodge the blows and protect himself but it was not possible.

For a second the puppy watched in stunned silence as all this happened — then attacked the man himself, trying to bite his leg. At first the man ignored this interference but finally pushed the dog away.

When the puppy came back the man stopped beating the boy and looked long and hard at the puppy. In what was almost a slow mo-tion picture of a football field goal hero his right leg moved back further and further then came forward. It caught the puppy right in the belly and sent him twenty feet into the air, far out into the ocean waves. Six eyes followed the flight. When the puppy disappeared into the water the grinning man began to drag the boy back toward the fence.

The path down to the beach was some distance away. It took me about five minutes to get there but I could find no sign of the puppy. I tried to figure out where the waves might have taken him. I walked the beach in both directions but over an hour's search left me with nothing.

I told the manager of the retreat house the story. He knew the man and boy at once. There had been complaints from neighbors for years about the way he treated his children but none of the kids would ever confirm that anything had happened. We called the local police. Nothing came from it.

The manager said that the puppy was probably a stray from one of the neighboring farms. It might never even be missed.

After a night of poor sleep I told my retreat director the story and how incredibly sad it made me feel. She thought for a few moments and then said, "Up there on that cliff you have never been more like God."

October 30, 1999

Knowing How To Be Right

Twenty years ago it was socially acceptable to smoke cigarettes in public but not to have had an abortion. Today smoking is a serious social sin while having an abortion has no social consequence whatever. That truth exemplifies the ineptitude of pro-life advocates on the one hand and the brilliance of the anti-smoking forces on the other.

Both groups saw a social evil and decided to fight against it. One – the anti-smoking forces – realized that they had to first educate people and social and legal changes would follow. They were right. The other group – the pro-life forces – chose to try to change the laws without any education of the people. They have failed totally.

It is not a matter of being right or wrong on the social issue involved [I think both groups are right], and it is not a matter of their opponents being stronger or better financed [big tobacco has much more money than pro-abortion forces]. The difference between success and failure was in the basic difference between knowing or not knowing <u>how to be right</u>.

As a member of the clergy this is a very important issue for me. I firmly believe in the teachings of my Church on moral and social issues. But I am constantly distressed by how often we may be right on the issues, but totally incompetent in effectively communicating our teaching. This is true not only of Catholicism but of almost all religious groups and churches.

When the Catholic Church teaches on a moral issue we usually publish a long complicated letter from the pope (called an encyclical) or a group of bishops (called a pastoral letter). Until very recently there was never an outline or synopsis provided, leaving to untrained reporters from public news agencies the responsibility for telling the world what is being said. A two paragraph newspaper story is never a totally accurate presentation of a letter dozens of pages long, but two paragraphs written by a reporter is the only explanation most people ever receive of detailed Church teaching.

This is what happened with the Church's teaching on artificial contraception in the encyclical *Humanae Vitae* in 1968. That very complicated, minutely detailed letter was reduced to the phrase "Pope says no to birth control." This distortion of the Church's actual teaching was not the fault of the press, it was the fault of the Church for not knowing how to accurately teach in the modern world of the media. That the passage of time has shown that the teaching may have indeed been right was well expressed in a *New York Times* news service article by Mike McManus reprinted in the October 24, 1999, issue of the *Bend Bulletin*. But being right in 1968 was not enough, the Church should have known how to be right.

The Catholic Church has done a very poor job of effectively communicating its teaching on almost all of the issues surrounding human life. We have a truly outstanding consistent teaching on the sacredness of all human life from the moment of conception to the right to die a natural death. We put capital punishment, physician assisted suicide, the exultation of choice, infanticide, abortion, sexism, racism, and all the other life issues into a logical and consistent perspective that shows the beauty and nobility of the human person. But in almost every public airing of these issues we do not know how to express this teaching in an effective manner. We may be right, but we don't know how to be right.

Other churches do not do much better. Those fundamentalist and bible-based churches which simply quote biblical passages and apply them to social issues are only effective with people who share their view of biblical absolutism. Most people just ignore these churches. Many of the main-stream Protestant churches have serious difficulties teaching about moral and social issues, lacking the absolutism of the fundamentalists or the authority structure of the Catholics.

There are major moral and social problems in our society, including all the life issues, drugs, greed, racism, soiled politics, genetic engineering and others. It is the responsibility of the churches and religious bodies in our society to identify and work to solve these problems. It is not enough to have great religious minds figure out the moral and ethical whats and whys of all these issues. It is not enough to write learned and painstakingly accurate papers and letters about them. It is not enough to find biblical passages that comment upon them.

Churches and religious bodies must also discover how to effectively communicate with (listen and talk) and accurately teach the public at large about these issues. In America laws reflect public opinion, and public opinion is formed by effective education and communication.

The abortion issue remains the outstanding example of being right but not knowing how to be right. As long as the pro-life forces, including the Catholic Church, spend most of their effort on working with politicians to change laws, abortion will be with us. The 1998-99 Respect Life Program of the Catholic Church does show some better efforts to accurately teach what abortion is and does, but it is not enough. The Church must also participate in honest dialogue on the causes of unwanted pregnancy, in order for we as a nation to finally find the ways to eliminate this terrible evil.

There are issues coming to the fore in American life where the churches and religious bodies could and should make a major difference. These include capital punishment, physician assisted suicide, infanticide, homosexuality, gay marriage, genetic engineering, the environment, etc. Some of these issues will appear at the ballot box, some will be debated in other forums.

If churches, including my own Catholic Church, wish to be involved in these debates, they must spend as much time figuring out how to express their teachings as they do determining what those teachings are. They do not serve society if they simply announce from on high what the magic answer is and assume people will listen to them. It just doesn't work that way.

Society has been much too tolerant of the churches' incompetence and unwillingness to effectively communicate moral and ethical teachings. Churches and church leaders should be held accountable for both the message and the means used to communicate that message. All churches and religious bodies need to learn that it is not enough to be right, it is equally important to know how to be right.

November 27, 1999

Personal Choice: A Pendulum Swung Too Far?

When future historians examine American culture in the last part of the twentieth century they will note the strong obsession with personal choice. They will write that beginning about 1973 the historic relationship between personal choice and the common good underwent a profound change in America. The pendulum swung so far to the side of choice that it went from being a relative value to an absolute value.

The individual person and the value of choice have always been an important part of American thought. Our Protestant civil heritage, our struggles with England, our ancestors being persons with the courage to cross the ocean and begin a new life – there are many reasons the individual person and the ability to make choices has always been so important to us as Americans. Throughout the world American freedom has always meant the ability to choose.

But both individualism and choice were never absolute values. They were always understood to exist in partnership with the idea of the common good. There was a marvelous intricate balance between the role and choice of the individual and the needs of the common good.

But in 1973, a specific event, and a great public relations campaign, transformed individualism and choice into the new and all powerful "personal choice." After the Roe vs Wade decision permitting abortion, it was obvious that there would be intense public disagreement. To control the coming debate the people who favored abortion made the decision (with the help of public relations experts) to shift the focus of the debate from abortion to "personal choice." It was a stroke of absolute genius.

"Personal choice" was redefined as an historic and constitutional right, and declared to be an absolute value. The specific issue of abortion was ignored because the issue was now a woman's right to choose. People who called themselves pro-life tried to talk about abortion but it was impossible to do so. There has never been an actual national debate because the two sides were talking (shouting) in totally different languages, neither capable of hearing the other.

What was discussed was if a person was pro-choice or anti-choice. A person's position on "choice" became the litmus test for American life, for politicians, for judges, for educators, for social events, for jobs. Many people, including many Catholics, found security in holding two intellectually incompatible positions – claiming to be both anti-abortion but pro-choice.

The massive effort to promote personal choice as an absolute value was successful beyond its creators' wildest dreams. It spread like wildfire. Its success cannot be blamed only on the issue of abortion, it was an idea whose time had come. Traditional values – love, respect, honesty, courage, patriotism – had become suspect during the 60's and the Vietnam war. Personal choice as an absolute value filled that void. Books, articles, interviews all trumpeted how fortunate we all were now that it had been identified. As an absolute value choice began to dominate areas where it had always been united to the common good.

Personal choice claimed that each person had the right to live life "my way." It uses phrases such as "it is my life", "it is my body," "leave me alone," and "the right to privacy." It became the basis for legal court decisions, passage of legislation, and especially the personal philosophies of millions of people. Baby books told parents they had to let their infants choose what they wanted, schools allowed students to choose what they learned, and, combined with the new birth control pill, society encouraged everyone to choose new social and sexual mores.

Personal choice has eclipsed substantive discussion about social issues including gun control, physician assisted suicide, medical marijuana use, and homosexuality. Once proponents focused the actual issue into a personal choice issue, the opportunities for serious dialogue were gone.

Personal choice as an absolute value has become so strong it overshadows the common good in much of American life. It is one of the major reasons for the incredible decline in American political life. With the value of the common good gone from politics the old enemies of good government — personal hatred, single issue politics, non-negotiables, lack of civility, immorality, unbridled ambition – now dominate both state and national governments.

It would not be possible for a modern politician to sincerely speak the words of John F. Kennedy's inaugural address – "ask not what your country can do for you but what you can do for your country." Someone saying that today would be laughed off the podium.

But personal choice is not equally available to all people. Because personal choice is really about control, strong people want to control themselves, and often want to control other people as well. The best example are the people who insist that a 15 year old girl can choose to get an abortion but equally insist that the same girl cannot choose to smoke a cigarette. The young, weak, poor and powerless are free to choose only what the strong want to allow them to choose.

There is also a failure to always connect personal responsibility with personal choice. Some people who make the personal choices to drive drunk, have an abortion, or own a gun, want someone else – the hospital, the government, the insurance company – to pay for any costs connected with their choices. The logic behind this is that personal choice is such an absolute right that all people must pay for other people's personal choices.

My own Catholic Church (and most other churches) is out of step with the new role of personal choice as an absolute value. We don't believe in absolute individualism or absolute choice. We do believe in the importance of the individual and the importance of choice, but always in partnership with the common good and the need for care for the most vulnerable members of society. What is absolute is the dignity and sanctity of human life from conception to death.

Thus for the Catholic Church and many other churches, a "woman's right to choose" is less important than the "child's right to life." Our belief in the common good forces us to try to defend the human lives of the unborn, the sick, the old, the guilty, and all others. We see all human life as so closely tied together that to kill one of us is to harm all of us.

People with personal choice as their highest value see churches, especially Catholicism, as trying to impose our morality on them. They see churches as strong people who are trying to control other people's freedom to choose. It is a legitimate fear. Churches in the past, including Catholicism, have sometimes denied legitimate freedoms and tried to control people's lives.

But the fact that we churches have made mistakes and even committed sins during our church history cannot be allowed to keep us from trying to do the right thing now. We who are involved in public debates about moral issues must constantly reexamine our positions to make sure we are not seeking to control other people's lives. Our goal must always be the common good and the defense of those who cannot defend themselves. We also have to accept the reality that as a Church we are out of step with much of our culture. We simply do not believe that personal choice is the highest human value.

The exaltation of personal choice into an absolute value has had many consequences in American life. The genie the pro-abortion forces let out of the bottle caused the pendulum between personal choice and the common good to swing far to one side. It is time for a serious dispassionate national discussion about the relationship between them. The churches must call for that debate and be part of it.

December 25, 1999

There Is A Lot Of Stuff At Christmas Which Doesn't Make Sense

We've got a lot of the facts wrong. We know that Jesus was not born in December, but probably in late spring; that he was not born in the year 1, but probably in 4 BC (which means the millennium actually happened four years ago); and that the magi, the star, the shepherds, the manger, the angel, the donkey, and all the other warm and wonderful parts of the Christmas story are very difficult to authenticate outside the Gospel stories.

We also know that by every standard of both his time and ours Jesus was a failure. He was basically an unemployed carpenter of questionable parentage who became a self-proclaimed traveling preacher. He gathered a ragtag group of fishermen and others followers, most of whom came from Galilee, the "hick country" of the little unimportant Roman province of Palestine. He got the self-righteous authorities upset and was killed as a common criminal.

He made no money, wrote no books, won no wars, and left no biological descendants. He did name a successor, a loud mouthed bumpkin fisherman nicknamed "Rocky" who when put to the test promptly denied even knowing him. And for most of the 2000 years since he lived, some of the people who claim to be his followers have argued, fought, and even killed each other about what he meant.

So what is the fascination with Christmas? Why do we retell this inaccurate and sometimes incorrect two thousand year old story of a peasant felon? Why do we stop our lives, our daily routines, and decorate our rooms with dead trees covered with colored lights and silly looking balls? Why do we buy presents which other people don't really need with money we don't really have? Why wasn't Ebenezer Scrooge right – "bah humbug!"

It all comes down to this thing about Jesus being God. For people who don't believe that Jesus is God who became a human being,

Christmas has no meaning at all. But for people who do believe that God so loved the world that he himself became one of us, all the messiness about the details of Jesus' life, the stupidity of his followers, and the sins of history only add to the mystery and the adventure.

It is truly fascinating that once a person has faith in Jesus, then all the parts of the story fall into place. What is important stands out as important – he was born, he lived, he preached, he healed, he died, he rose, he founded his Church, he ascended to the father. What isn't important fades into curiosity and observations – the date of his birth, the size of the star, the menu at the last supper. The immaturity and incompetence of the apostles only increases the miracle that the Church grew and prospered. The sinfulness of twenty centuries of followers proves that only a divine Church could have survived.

This faith in Jesus as God become human is not always an easy thing to achieve or keep. If it is true faith it raises so many questions, causes so much serious thinking. The biggest question is also the most simple – Why? Why would God, perfectly happy for all eternity, decide to create humanity and cause himself so much grief? And why would God choose to become one of those humans? Why would God choose such a terrible time in history and such a difficult place and people? Why would God allow himself to be put to death? Why would he bother to rise again, what would that gain him? The fundamental question is always "why?" and there are not always adequate answers.

I don't have final answers to all those questions; no one does. There is something about the whole God/Jesus story which remains just outside the world of answers, something real but intangible, able to be touched but never grasped. At the end of his life when St. John the Evangelist tried to get it down on paper he could only say that "God is love." It has probably never been said better.

God loves us, both individually and collectively. He loves us so much that he became one of us. Some of us feel and respond to that love, some of us feel it but choose not to respond, and some of us never even feel it. I think a lot of the difference is whether or not we see ourselves as needing God's love.

When he was asked why he came to earth Jesus went back in Jewish scripture and quoted Isaiah: "The spirit of the Lord is upon me; therefore he has anointed me. He has sent me to bring glad tidings to the poor, to proclaim liberty to captives, recovery of sight to the blind, and release to prisoners, to announce a year of favor from the Lord." (Luke 4:18-19)

God became a human being for five reasons, all dealing with the poor, the captives, the blind, prisoners, and the need for a year of favor. I will not find God unless I am poor and listening for the glad tidings, unless I am a captive hoping for liberty. I will not experience God unless I am blind needing sight, unless I am a prisoner needing release.

Every time I think I am a rich self-made man or totally free on my own merits, or think I can see through my own efforts or that I am better than others, I begin to slowly ebb away from my relationship with Jesus, with God, my faith weakens, and my sinfulness grows. But every time I come back to reality, and see things as they really are, then my faith grows, and I find myself enjoying life too much to sin.

Jesus only makes sense to the poor, the blind, the captive, the prisoners. And it is a sense beyond intelligence, beyond reason, beyond science, it is a sense which is grounded in faith, in hope, and especially in love.

To the poor and the blind it makes sense to drag a dead tree into the house and put all sorts of stuff on it, to buy presents, to send cards, because that tree, those presents, those cards are ways of saying thank you for the glad tidings and for the gift of sight. To prisoners and captives it makes sense that Jesus choose Peter as his successor because Peter was a captive to his own emotions, fears, and sin, and Jesus gave him the liberty and release of forgiveness.

Christmas is beyond making sense. It is a time for people to enjoy God and each other.

February 12, 2000

Who Has The Right To End A Human Life?

He is a man now, in his early twenties. When he shot the store owner he was sixteen. The evidence was overwhelming, and he was convicted of murder and sentenced to death. Hundreds of people who have never met him have rallied to his defense, begging that he not be killed. Hundreds of other people, including some of the murdered man's relatives, want him executed. There are demonstrations, letters from religious leaders including the pope. Politicians gage the political wind and give the current popular view as their own. Everyone claims the high moral ground, absolutely incapable of understanding how those in the opposite camp could be so totally wrong.

That is a fictional story, but based on numerous real examples. Just as the debate about the right to life and abortion has dominated the last thirty years of the last century in American life, so the wider right to life question of capital punishment and state execution will come to dominate the first decades of this new century. It will be a much more contentious, fractious and ugly national struggle than the abortion issue has been.

The initial sides seem uneven. Americans have an international reputation for supporting, even relishing, the right to execute. Every execution gives us pictures of relatives of the murder victim claiming that they will only feel good again when "justice is done" and the convicted killer is himself dead. The camera angles and sound clips make the relatives appear to be more a pack of salivating animals anxious for the kill than real human beings. The press street interviews during executions inevitably have car mechanic saying, "Fry 'em," and short haired, well dressed lawyers talking about how executions are effective deterrents.

On the pro-life side there is often a long haired, poorly dressed lawyer talking about how the killer had a terrible childhood, was abused, but has now changed and deserves to live. There is usually some member of the clergy or a nun standing in the background.

The whole group looks like a 60's anti-war campaign or a 70's rally trying to save the whales.

Those who want death almost always win, especially if the decision is up to an elected official. The Bush brothers as governors in Texas and Florida have become famous for the number of executions they have approved. Anti-death people have little political clout as the abortion and physician assisted suicide issues have shown.

But there is a pro-life anti-execution momentum beginning to build. Some states have begun to debate the effectiveness and even the morality of the death penalty. Movies – "Dead Man Walking" and "The Green Mile" – have raised new questions. The number of prisoners sentenced to death who have been proven innocent by DNA is staggering, and calls into question the morality of the entire prosecution and conviction juggernaut that has come to be the norm in much of the American legal system. That is especially apparent when the defendant is poor.

The right to life/abortion debate was co-opted by a specific form of feminism into a public relations campaign about choice, effectively denying the American people the opportunity to ever really discuss abortion. It can only be hoped that that the same will not happen, and that there will be a true right to life/execution national debate.

The sides of such a debate about right to life/execution are not yet clear. One side will be the relatives of victims and victims rights groups. They will play an important role, justifiably asking for punishment for those who murdered their family members. But they will increasingly be challenged to explain how killing another person brings them relief from their sorrow. That victims relatives can find joy and satisfaction in another person's death is itself going to become an issue. The promoters of the deterrent theory are going to be challenged by people who simply say it does not prove true.

The anti-death side will be a combination of pragmatists and moralists. The pragmatists will argue that execution is both unfair and financially more costly than life imprisonment. State execution has too much danger of killing innocent people, and is simply bad business. These will be the people who will have the statistics.

The moralists will have a more difficult time. There is a presumption that those sentenced to execution are guilty. That might not be true, or it might be only somewhat true. But our popular culture is not good at distinctions or mitigating factors. There is the perceived need for punishment, and there is the impression that the only two options are death or "getting away with it." Prisons have been presented by campaigning politicians as country clubs with weight rooms and cable TV, so life in prison even without the possibility of parole is viewed as some type of lifetime vacation at Club Med. That is a hard image for a moralist to change.

The whole debate will be most difficult for the churches, especially the Roman Catholic Church. Catholics, even Catholic clergy, have been overwhelmingly in favor of the death penalty. It is Pope John Paul II who has forced this issue into the Catholic understanding of the sacredness of life. He has joined the late Cardinal Bernadin of Chicago in teaching of a seamless garment of life, viewing all life as sacred from conception until natural death.

Officially the Catholic Church both universally and specifically in the United States is clearly on record opposing the death penalty. According to Catholic teaching, execution (with extremely rare exception) is not something a country can morally do. Unofficially that teaching is hotly debated both by clergy and laity.

Those fighting abortion worry that expanding the church's teaching on life as the Pope is doing will water down the fight against abortion. Since moral theologians many years ago taught that executions were moral, many older priests find it difficult to see how they can now be seen as immoral. And there are a number of Catholic laity who have always subscribed to the "fry 'em" theory of justice. They do not want their mindsets challenged.

Oregon will hopefully have an initiative about right to life/execution on the November ballot. Oregonians have a history now of favoring death over life on social issues. That history is up once again for re-evaluation. The Catholic Church in Oregon will take a stand on the issue, just as it did on the right to life/suicide issue. Hopefully this time the people of Oregon will choose life over death, even for those convicted of crime.

The bottom line issue is: "Who has the right to end a human life – of an unborn child, of a handicapped person, of one's self, of a convicted criminal?" One side says that only God has that right because all life is sacred. The other side says that life is not sacred and that individuals have the right to kill other individuals (abortion) or help individuals kill themselves (assisted suicide) or the state can choose people to kill (capital punishment).

March 4, 2000

Welcome To Ash Wednesday

He walked into the church boldly, looked at the holy water font but passed it by without blessing himself and settled into a pew toward the back. Mass on Ash Wednesday had just begun. He listened to the readings, even stood for the Gospel and by instinct blessed his forehead and lips before he realized what he was doing. He sat for the homily and then got in line for ashes. He walked to the front, bowed his head, and was marked for the beginning of Lent. He didn't stay for the rest of Mass.

Now there is nothing too remarkable about this for some people, but this man was a prominent ex-Catholic, now fundamentalist, and quite an anti-Catholic Church leader in town. I was the pastor and recognized him. I thought about it and then phoned him. I simply said I had seen him and wanted him to know he was always welcome.

He laughed and said that he had rejected everything about Catholicism and didn't believe any of it, adding a tidbit or two about the "Whore of Babylon" and the pope as the anti-Christ. Then he said, "But the one thing I miss is ashes on Ash Wednesday, so I come and get them. It is the one thing you people do right."

The power of ashes on Ash Wednesday never ceases to amaze me. On this coming Wednesday an endless variety of people will walk down church aisles and have ashes placed on their heads with words like "Remember that you are dust and to dust you will return" or "Repent and hear the good news." Cops in uniforms will be next to kids with purple hair. Older proper ladies will be next to young giggling girls.

Ashes is one of those things open to everyone – Catholic, Protestant, Jewish, Moslem, Hindu, atheist, and all others. Mardi Gras revelers who have yet to go to bed, come and get ashes along side those who ate the pancake supper at the local Episcopal Church. Men, women, boys, girls, old, young, Mexican, Irish, Native American, Italian, Japanese – there is something about getting ashes that goes beyond all age and ethnic lines.

I had a friend whose tough New York parish was the place where the whores and strippers, male and female, came and stood in the back of the church so they could get ashes on Ash Wednesday. There are people who need to feel that there is a place they can come to, a place they belong. The street people, the rent boys, the ladies of the night, these are the people who need to feel God stills loves them and welcomes them home, no matter how infrequently they come. Even the little simple thing of receiving ashes can be the one tie between a bitter past and better future.

Now the hope and prayer of course is that the reception of ashes is a sign of a true and sincere desire for change. The person receiving ashes is proclaiming that he or she is going to do something in the coming weeks of Lent. But even if they do not fulfill that hope this year or next, the simple desire for change will someday lead them to find the grace and courage to change.

Many of the people who come for ashes on Ash Wednesday are not Catholics, but the majority of them have some connection with the Catholic Church.

There is a famous statistic that the largest single religious group in America is practicing Catholics, and the second largest is non-practicing Catholics. That is abundantly true in Central Oregon, where estimates range as high as 30% of the famous "un-churched" are non-practicing Catholics. Some of these people will go to Church only on Easter or Christmas, a few others only on Palm Sunday. But many of them will come only on Ash Wednesday.

Some of those non-practicing Catholics are men who married a woman in a Protestant church. At the time they weren't going to the Catholic church. After a few years and a few children, their wives convince them that everyone needs to go to church together as a family. This is of course the wives' Protestant church, and the husbands might even join. But as they get older, they miss some of Catholicism, and they realize there is one day a year when they sneak off and get ashes. It is something they need to do.

It used to be the custom to wipe off the ashes as soon as you received them, but today it is preferred to keep them on all day long, letting everyone see them. The once-a-year people wipe them off very quickly, but it was still important to get them.

In some places in the country there are priests who get upset that some people only come to church once or twice a year, or that they come and get ashes but then never show up again until next year. Priests like that irritate me. They do more harm than good. Just because someone doesn't fit into the regular mold at this point in his or her life, they are made to feel condemned. Many of those ex-Catholics have stories about spiritual abuse at the hands of priests like that.

The rest of us priests rejoice that people know that no matter what they have done or where their own particular journey has taken them, that they are always welcome, even if it is just for ashes on Ash Wednesday.

This coming Wednesday is Ash Wednesday. Everyone is welcome.

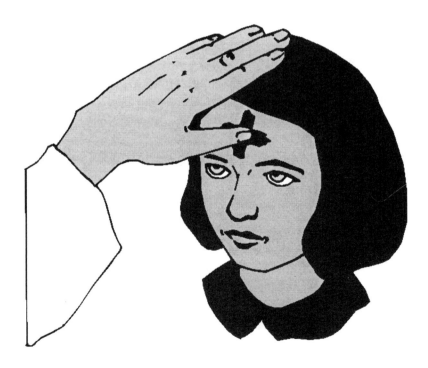

April 22, 2000

What Actually Happens In The Miracle Of Baptism?

Easter begins with the lighting of the Easter Fire. In the liturgical churches this fire symbolizes the triumph of light over darkness which is exactly what the resurrection of Jesus Christ is. But during the great Easter Vigil and First Mass of Easter the main symbolism changes from fire to water. For this night is the night when those who have been preparing for Baptism have their desire fulfilled.

From the earliest days of the Church adults have been baptised at the Easter Vigil on Holy Saturday night. This is the greatest night in all the Church year, the night on which we relive the great moments of our salvation, and no time could be more appropriate for the great event of Baptism.

This is the theory, the theology contained in church teaching. But what really is Baptism? What is it that is happening to the thousands of men and women who are reborn in the blessed water at the Easter Vigil? Let me do a little explaining and then answer these two questions.

As is the case with so much of Christianity, the meaning of Baptism differs in major ways along the spectrum of churches and denominations. At the fundamentalist end of the Protestant tradition Baptism is more or less just a symbol of the Resurrection in which the individual dies to the old self and rises to the new. It can even be repeated many times if needed. Baptism is not very important because what really matters is the moment when an individual chooses to accept Jesus Christ as his/her personal savior. Other Protestant denominations have other explanations of what Baptism is.

At the Catholic and Orthodox end of the spectrum Baptism is extremely important. It is a monumental action of God. It is not just something an individual does but it is also something done to the Church as well as by the Church.

Catholics understand that human beings are born with a need for God, a spiritual void inside of them which only the presence of God

118

can fill. The purpose of life is to fill that void with God. When God comes into us, becomes part of us, we identify God by the name grace. A person is only truly complete, is only truly a full human being when he or she has chosen to receive God's grace, and begins the journey in life of growing more and more like God.

Thus life is a journey, the purpose of which is to let God into us so that we may be complete. But [and it is here that the Protestant and Catholic traditions go in very different directions] Catholics believe that no one is alone on this journey. We are not just individuals accepting God, we are also a community of people accepting God. Not only does each individual have a God shaped void, but the community has a God shaped void. So the community is also accepting God. This community we call the Church, and the people who are the Church share God's grace with one another.

The best analogy is that of a family. Each member of a family is an individual, but each is also an essential part of the family. Being part of the family helps tell each person who he or she is. In the same way, an individual who is part of the Church is more than just an individual, he or she is the Church.

Thus for Catholics and Orthodox, Baptism is how an individual person goes beyond his or her individuality and becomes Church. By Baptism the person receives God, becomes one with God, is filled with God's grace. And by Baptism the person becomes Church and the Church is forever changed by the addition of one more person who is now Church for all eternity.

Baptism is an event of the journey of life. For some people it is the beginning, for others it is deep into the journey. But for everyone it is the moment when the journey is changed forever. The individual is no longer just an individual but is an essential element of Church. Some of the other names of Church show this even more clearly, such as the People of God and the Mystical Body of Christ.

At one point we talked about all of this using negative language, especially the phrase "original sin." Original sin was an easier way of saying that we are born in need of God, and of explaining the consequences of not having God. It also explained what happens when God come into someone's life. There is nothing at all wrong with using the words "original sin," after all they come from St. Augustine and have been used for years in Christian tradition. But using a negative concept like original sin to explain a wonderful and positive reality such as Baptism is self-defeating. It makes so much more sense to explain things positively rather than negatively.

So what really is Baptism? Baptism is a sacrament [a physical action created by God] by which an individual unites him/herself with God and with all the other people who have God within them. It is permanent, it lasts forever, it makes someone who he or she is. Original sin and all sins are forgiven in Baptism because when God comes there is no room for sin and evil. Future sins will be forgiven in the sacrament of Penance.

And our second question was what is it that is happening to the thousands of men and women who are reborn in the blessed water at the Easter Vigil? They cease to be just individuals, they have God and other people as part of their lives. They are on a journey to fill themselves up with God, to become like God, to eventually see God face to face. It is not just an individual journey, it is a communal journey. And it is a life long journey, made even more exciting and wonderful by the other six sacraments.

The same thing happens with an infant or child who is baptised. Parents have God within them by their Baptism. They have ceased to be just individuals and become part of Church, and they yearn to share this gift with their child. Having God become part of a child's life and having the child become an essential part of Church is the greatest gift they can give the child. It is pure love.

All of the theology of Baptism makes sense only if it is seen as the act by which someone becomes more than just an individual and becomes part of the People of God, the Mystical Body of Christ, the Church. It then becomes the most important step on the journey.

From Baptism onward, the person is never alone. He or she can never be unbaptised, it can never be erased. I remember the old phrase, "Once a Catholic, always a Catholic," from my childhood. It is totally true. Once a person is part of the Church, then the Church is always a part of that person. God and the community are with each person no matter what he/she does, no matter how far he/she may wander, no matter how much he/she may even reject God or the community.

Easter is so special because of both the death and rising of Christ, and because it is the time when the Church is renewed and refreshed by all the great and good people who become one with us. Jesus Christ is Risen and he brings us with him. Alleluia!

April 29, 2000

A Very Difficult
Column To Write

This has been a difficult column to write. I started it about four months ago. I've finished it about six times, only to go back and change it. The difficulty is that I want to write about the concept of "life" in a way that people who do not agree with me will still read it and respond to it. I strongly believe that we humans are increasingly treating life as having little or no value. The three great examples of this here in Oregon are abortion, physician assisted suicide, and capital punishment.

I am convinced that we need much more honest dialogue and debate about the issue of life. But since all three of those actions are presently legal, people who favor them do not want a discussion or dialogue. They wish people like me would just shut up and go away. But the issue is too important for me to do that.

There are two main points I want to raise to begin some type of discussion or dialogue. The first is the issue of individual persons choosing criteria for who can live or die, the second is the refusal to discuss the actual act of abortion itself.

There are individuals who create their own criteria for deciding who can live or die. Some persons' criteria are ethnic, others educational, others personal, others inconvenience, still others pain or loss of control. But once an individual chooses to have personal subjective criteria to determine who can live or die, then any one person's criteria are as valid as anyone else's. I cannot see any difference between someone who is willing to kill another person because he or she is ethnically different (e.g. Jewish or Albanian) and someone who is willing to kill someone who is still in the womb (e.g. abortion) or who has been convicted of a crime (e.g. capital punishment.) Once someone decides that he or she can have his or her own personal life/death criteria, a line has been crossed. From that point on, it is only a matter of what criteria are chosen.

Because most people advocating abortion, capital punishment and suicide are basically good people, such a comparison is consid-

121

ered offensive by them. I am sorry about that, and I don't mean to offend, but I think the comparison is valid. If it is not valid, I would like to know why not.

My second point is the refusal of people who favor abortion to discuss abortion. They always want to talk about choice. I think this is the major reason that having honest discussion and debate about life is so difficult.

Choice and abortion are two very different things. Choice is a decision. Choice is something which takes place in the mind. It is a mental exercise. A television show about choice is *Who wants to be a Millionaire?* Choice is blinking lights, bells, whistles and Regis Philbin.

Abortion is a medical procedure. A living fetus inside the womb is extracted and the life of the fetus is terminated. A television show about abortion would show a doctor and medical equipment and blood and body tissue. No bells, no whistles, no Regis.

Choice and abortion are two very different issues, both of which deserve discussion. But when any attempt to discuss abortion arises, someone immediately says, "The issue here is a woman's right to choose," and from that point on abortion is never discussed.

There is certainly room for good discussion about choice and choices. So many things about a pregnancy call for decisions. And each decision has consequences and all of those need to be looked at and evaluated. Issues like unwanted pregnancy, child abuse, rape, incest, all the social context questions surrounding pregnancy – these need a full public airing.

But there is also a need for good discussion about abortion. What is an abortion? What is a fetus? What is being aborted? What physically happens to the pregnant woman? What difference does it make how far along the pregnancy is? And finally the big question – Is the fetus a living human being? If so, why? If not, why not?

And if it is a living human being, is aborting the fetus the same as killing a person? If so, why? If not, why not? Is a living human being a person? If so, why? If not, why not?

These are the questions which have been kept from being discussed for the last thirty years because every time they are raised someone says, "No, we can't talk about those things because the issue here is a woman's right to choose." When someone asks, "If she chooses abortion, what does that mean?" The answer comes back, "We can't talk about abortion because the issue is a woman's right to choose."

I don't blame those who favor abortion for using this strategy. It has been incredibly effective at keeping the discussion from ever actually looking at the physical or psychological aspects of the medical procedure, much less looking at the issue of whether or not the aborted fetus was really a living human being, was really a person.

Most people who favor abortion are good people who see it as the remedy for social evils. Most of them can remember a case of this person or that one who got pregnant and "to have the baby would have ruined their life" or "the baby wasn't perfect" or "they couldn't afford it" or some other good reason. If they truly believed the fetus was a living human person they couldn't support abortion. It is absolutely essential to strong abortion proponents that the question of whether or not the fetus is a living human person never be discussed. By always making the discussion about choice, they make sure they can always get support for abortion.

Other ways to never actually discuss what abortion really is are to make "reproductive rights" a woman's issue [which is what the Democratic Party has done], or portraying abortion opponents as crazed right wing religious fanatics [that some right to life advocates are blatant murderers themselves makes that argument easier].

The issue of the meaning of life is not going to go away, and it has to eventually be dealt with. Physician assisted suicide has been on the ballot twice and is before the US congress now; capital punishment may well be on the ballot soon; and abortions are taking place on a regular basis in Bend. These issues touch people's lives. Local medical practices have been dissolved over the abortion debate. People are in jail at the north end of Bend while downtown prosecutors strategize seeking their deaths. Area pharmacists and hospice workers have been forced to face the issue of getting pills to use to kill someone.

These two points — the issue of people deciding criteria for life and death and the refusal of abortion proponents to discuss the actual act of abortion itself – are two small drops into the ocean of discussion and debate which needs to happen. It is my hope that the people who favor abortion, capital punishment, and suicide will not hide behind the fact that their positions are presently legal in Oregon but will come out and get involved in real discussion on these issues.

Such discussion needs to be respectful on the part of all the people involved. It will take true listening, true openness to points of view alien to the listener. It cannot be filled with name calling and rancor. It might well make use of discussion techniques such as "Common Ground" offered by Interfaith Ministries of Central Oregon.

There are communities in the United States where real discussion has taken place on the abortion issue. They are few and far between, but they do exist. This means it can be done. But it takes people who think the issues are important enough to spend time talking about them, and important enough to be civil and polite when doing so.

Three major life issues – abortion, capital punishment, suicide – cut across our community and our state. They are not going to go away. They need to be discussed.

May 27, 2000

Does Sex Have Anything To Do With Morality?

We live in a world and society with an incredible breadth of sexual variation. By this I mean sex within marriage, sex outside of marriage, sex before marriage, multiple partner sex, solo sex, homosexuality, lesbianism, various types of intercourse, various ages for partners, various partners for sex, and the list could go on and on. We have a sex industry growing at a phenomenal rate on the web, in videos, in magazines, with pornography accepted as a legitimate occupation.

The various sexual infidelities of the president and other politicians are viewed by society as having no special importance. Living together is considered normal not only for the young but for couples of all ages.

The various Christian denominations, including my own Catholicism, have a difficult time dealing with the morality of these sexual issues. Churches and denominations take various approaches. One extreme is to totally evade the subject and never talk about it at all. The other is to have a detailed listing of every possible sexual activity with a corresponding judgement about the rightness or wrongness of each. Most Christian bodies take some type of position between these extremes.

Historically much of the Christian approach to sex is expressed in terms from the theological writing of Saint Augustine of Hippo, once a notorious libertine who later in life took a very dim view of all aspects of sex. Saint Augustine was not the first to apply moral judgements to sexual acts, God himself did that in the scriptures, but Augustine did set a tone which has profoundly influenced the last fifteen hundred years.

Part of that tone is the heavy emphasis on sin as the consequence of immoral sexual activity. This emphasis has often caused churches to begin the discussion of sex as a discussion of sin. For example, in many church groups and religion classes young people were told that masturbation and sex outside of marriage were sinful – end of topic. There was no real explanation of why those activities were considered immoral, just the statement that they were.

Among the problems with this approach are 1) sex and sin are automatically tied together. Sexual activity was said to be always sinful except marital intercourse which was never sinful. This is a totally negative approach. And 2) all aspects of sex are assumed to mean genital sexual activity. There was no mention or understanding of sexuality, sexual orientation, or other aspects of the human person as a sexual being.

My own Catholicism was very much part of this type of teaching. Official Catholicism has always taught that a mortal sin took three elements – serious matter, sufficient reflection, and full consent of the will. Unfortunately in far too many cases priests and sisters mistaught church teaching and said that all serious matter, such as sex outside of marriage, were always mortal sins, forgetting the other two conditions.

Obviously something is not right with the way sexual morality has been taught or the sexual revolution and the sexual culture we live in would not have developed. Many people simply dismiss morality from sex. I recently read an interview with a pornstar who also works as an escort paid to have sex with his clients. This well educated, intelligent, college graduate said he views sex as just another human activity, speaking about it as one would speak about playing basketball. He likes it, he's good at it, and he gets paid for it. When the interviewer asked him if there were any moral aspects to sex, the man said there were none.

Now we can say this pornstar is the exception, but I don't think he is that unusual. I think there are many Americans of all ages who see sex and morality as having no connection.

Ironically this is happening just as the morality and legality of hinting, speaking, and suggesting sex are on the front burner of popular culture. There is much more interest in the morality of sexual harassment than the morality of sexual activity.

I think it is a terrible mistake to separate sexual activity from morality. But I also think that the starting point for the discussion of the morality of sexuality activity cannot be sin. Morality and sin are not the same thing, and beginning any discussion with sin is a failed useless approach. I also think that the discussion of sex has to be much broader than simply genital sexual activity and open up all aspects of sexuality, including sexual orientation.

A discussion of the morality of sex should begin with what is good, beautiful, holy, and healthy about sexuality and then from that foundation move on to genital sexual activity. It should begin with a realization that a good and loving God created men and women as sexual beings, and also created sexual activity. Humanity is to enjoy our sexuality, take both joy and pleasure from our sexuality, and find God in our sexuality. The celebration of God's gift of sexuality does not necessarily have to include genital sexual activity. A person does not have to be having sex to be sexual.

But when a person does have sexual activity, what ideally makes that activity good, beautiful, holy, and healthy is the committed love between the man and woman who are having sex. It is a realization that the act is truly an act of love, with each endeavoring to bring joy and pleasure to their partner, an act open to the possibility that their love could literally become a new person. In the act of love between a man and woman publically committed to each other for life, they literally share God with one another, for God is love. Sex in this way is self-constructive and other-constructive behavior.

With that ideal starting point, sexuality and sexual activity can be seen for the incredible creations they are. Now there are ways of being sexual and forms of sexual activity which vary slightly from this ideal, or deviate quite a bit from this ideal, or are very distant from this ideal. There are forms of sexual activity in which love is not found, and God is not found. There are forms of sexual activity which are not self-constructive or other-constructive but self-destructive and other-destructive.

The further an act of sex is from the ideal, the more self-destructive it is. Sin is best defined as self-destructive behavior. Sex can be an generous act of love for another or a selfish act of love for self. Even in marriage sex can be a tool of hurt and pain, and therefore be sinful. Not all acts of sexual intercourse within marriage are automatically moral.

What makes an act of sexual activity good or sinful is whether or not it is an act of life giving love in which God is shared between the two people. The sadness of our culture is that for many people an act which should be a source of God is anything but that.

I did not find the pornstar's views disgusting, just terribly sad. He has taken those aspects of his life which could be a source of joy, peace, love, and God – his sexuality and his sexual activity – and made them into something which at most can give him some momentary pleasure and a few bucks. It makes no difference if the pornstar is gay or straight, he is wasting his life. The purpose of his life is to find and fill himself with God, and he is going the opposite direction.

Most of the people I know who enjoy good healthy sex within their marriage lives are good, joy filled, holy people, with a tendency to be generous. Most of the people I know who have frantic sex lives with various partners, are sad and lonely, with a tendency to be selfish. All of that is no coincidence.

God gave us the gift of human sexuality. That is where our teaching about sex has to begin, pointing out all that is good. The ideal of sexual activity is found in marital intercourse. Then we need to say that the further we are from that ideal in sex, the more harm we do to ourselves. We control whether or not our sexuality and our sexual activity bring us joy, holiness, peace, and love. If they do not, then we need to make some serious changes.

June 24, 2000

We Become Like The God We Worship

"We become like the God we worship." I first came across that concept in a slightly different form while reading the papers from a symposium on the breakdown of the American criminal justice system (more about that below). My subsequent reading lead me a book by the Linns – Dennis, Sheila, and Matthew – called *Good Goats*, where I learned even more.

It's true. We do become like the God we worship. People I know who have an image of a loving and kind God are loving, those who see God as firm, unyielding and severe are depressing, those whose God hates certain people hate those people themselves, and those who have no God often have no real center to their lives.

There are many images of God, especially in Christianity. We create these images from our understanding of the scriptures, from our experience, and especially from the ideas we were given as children. Just a few examples show this.

Some people worship The Alligator God who is mean, demanding and unforgiving. This God lies in wait for us to make a simple mistake, a simple error, a little sin, and then The Alligator God pounces on us, rips us to pieces, and says, "You're worthless, you're dirt, you're nothing but a stupid sinner. You are so lucky I am willing to save you, but you certainly don't deserve it."

There is an even more disturbing version, The Sadistic God. This is the God of hellfire and brimstone sermons who regrets his creation of humanity. This God created us just so we would fail his impossible tests and then he could send almost all of us to hell. Among the most popular images of God in America, The Sadistic God takes perverse joy in inflicting punishment.

There are people who worship The Cotton Candy God who simply goes around loving everyone and everything. This God makes no judgement, has no opinion, is more like a genius on drugs than a divine entity.

There is The Clockmaker God, remote and distant from humanity, who set the world in motion and has gone on to different things, not really giving any thought or care to us. This God's main attribute is benign indifference.

There is The Cheerleader God who is strong, loving and wise. This God wants us to succeed in everything we do. He is not interested in our sins but in the forgiveness of our sins.

This list of Gods could go on and on. What happens is that from all the various influences each of us creates a personal image of God. Slowly, as we pray, think, read our image of God becomes stronger and we begin to assume the attributes we think God has. We personally consciously and unconsciously become like the God we worship. We also do this as a nation, becoming like our national civic image of God.

If we think of God as loving, we try to be more loving. If we think of God as severe, we try to be more severe. If we think of God as merciful or just or forgiving or demanding we take on those qualities.

It is important that we know what God we admire and what God we are beginning to resemble? Take this little inventory:

1) What are the four main attributes of the God I believe in?

2) Can I see (and others see) those attributes in my own life?

3) How much does my God resemble (or is opposite from) my father or mother?

4) Does my God prefer to forgive or punish?

5) Does my God have a long memory, especially for hurts?

6) Do I treat my family members (spouse, parents, children, siblings) like God treats me?

7) Can my God change? Can I change?

8) Is my image of God the same as or different from the image held by the people around me?

We then need to stop and ask: Is this the God I want to worship? Is this the person I want to become?

The ramifications of the truth that we become like the God we worship are many. Issues such as abortion, war and peace, hunger, poverty, drugs, marriage, homosexuality are very influenced by our personal God and our American civic God. One of these issues is that we as a nation have created a prison system based on The Sadistic God who believes that crime is sin, and sin should be punished rather than forgiven. Next month in my column I want to look at that system.

W. Thomas Faucher

Saturday, July, 29, 2000

Our Prison System Is Based On A Sadistic Vengeful Image Of God

Last month I wrote about the reality that "We become like the God we worship." In that column I said that we each choose various attributes, ways of thought, characteristics and create our personal image of God. We then try consciously and unconsciously to take on those attributes ourselves. Our image of God may or may not reflect what God actually is like, but it is what we think God is like. I used five examples of personal images of God – the alligator God, the sadistic God, the cotton candy God, the cheerleader God, and the clockmaker God.

This month I want to talk about how there is also a plural image of God which we as a nation resemble. There is a very powerful force in the country called American civic religion. That religion projects our national image of God.

Our American civic God blesses the good with abundance but punishes the bad with poverty. The civic God is a male Christian image of God with some specific characteristics. This God is the remote all-seeing-eye God on our dollar bills, the (non-Jewish, non-Catholic, non-Hindu, non-Moslem) God prayed to in public schools, the partisan God used as a weapon by everyone in politics, the white sadistic God blessing those who massacred American Indians, the racist God of KKK cross burnings.

This national God made a dramatic appearance at a recent symposium on the US Penal System sponsored by the Washington DC based Woodstock Theological Center (of which I used to be an associate fellow). The point of the meeting was that the American criminal justice system does not work, exemplified by a 70 percent recidivism rate for juveniles and a 63 percent rate for adults.

The system failure comes from our national choice to make prisons places of punishment rather than rehabilitation. We have a na-

131

tional addiction to punishment because our prison system is founded on theology rather than psychology or sociology.

Simply put, because the overwhelming image of God in American civic religion is a demanding, vengeful God much more interested in punishment than forgiveness, we have created a prison system which reflects this theology. (We become like the God we worship.) Many if not most Americans think that all crime is sinful. Since a vengeful God requires that all sin be punished, then all crime must be punished – and the harder the better.

This brings into focus the fundamental question – what is the purpose of prison? If the purpose is to help the criminal not commit a crime again, then prisons are rehabilitative. If the purpose is to make the criminal suffer pain, then prisons are for punishment. Because the goal of our American criminal justice system is to punish rather than rehabilitate we are told that our present system works well. The fact that two thirds of the people in the system return proves that no rehabilitation has taken place. Return prisoners also fuel the very profitable prison industry.

Our vengeful sadistic American civic God demands punishment for the criminal, the sinner. There is no call for, no room for, no interest in forgiveness in the American criminal justice system. In all of American history there are few if any examples where the national "God of our Fathers" is a forgiving God.

It is this mentality that creates mandatory prison sentences, takes the school and drug programs out of prisons, does away with the prison library, eliminates physical exercise, and salivates at the death penalty. This mentality says, "Punish for the sake of inflicting pain." Our criminal justice system is theologically, sociologically and psychologically bankrupt. But it is our system and we just keep building more and more prisons for the sake of punishing people because that is what the civic American God wants us to do.

If punishment were viewed as merely the means to an end, and the end was the goal of having the criminal not commit another crime, then our criminal justice system would be very different. Any and all means to rehabilitate the person would be used. For some people prison might be appropriate, for others maybe education, or a drug program, the list could go on and on. But to think of real rehabilitation can only come from a truly heretical thought – sin and crime do not always need to be punished.

Followers of a loving God believe that sin and crime do not always need to be punished. Punishment is only one of many options, and usually the least effective. Jesus forgave sinners, he didn't punish them.

Followers of God the Sadist believe that sin and crime must always be punished – and they control our nation. The national glee at each death penalty execution is proof of that, especially with the certainty that from the moment of death every executed criminal will be burning eternally in hell. Only God the Sadist would create a hell like that, where those deserving forgiveness are denied it.

Could America have a criminal justice system based on hope of rehabilitation, a system where the goal was to help the criminal rather than punish the criminal? Probably not. Our system will not change as long as our national image of God is the sadistic, racist, unforgiving God we have inherited from our national ancestors.

If there is to be change, it can only begin when we ask ourselves some tough questions: 1) What is the purpose of prison? 2) Why do 2/3 of ex-convicts return? 3) Do I believe in, and am I beginning to resemble, a God who is more interested in pain and punishment than rehabilitation and forgiveness? 4) Does every criminal (every sinner) need to be punished? 5) What is the purpose of punishment?

We will have exactly the criminal justice system we want and deserve. In fact we do now.

August 26, 2000

Sexual Abuse Of Children By Catholic Priests

One of the saddest aspects of my twenty nine years as a Catholic priest has been the scandals connected with the sexual abuse of children by members of the Catholic clergy. In the last twenty years these sins and the reactions to them have substantially altered the Catholic Church and the lives of each priest in America.

To correctly see the clergy abuse issue it is necessary to understand how the abuse usually becomes known. Some years after the abuse took place a person, male or female, becomes aware of having been abused by a Catholic priest. Either directly or through a lawyer the victim contacts the local Catholic bishop. The bishop begins an investigation of the allegations. As a result of the investigation the church responds to the allegations.

The result of the investigation of allegations of abuse often follows a pattern. It exposes that there had been complaints or rumors about the priest. He was called into the office of whoever was bishop at that time for a confrontation. The bishop usually consulted as broadly as possible with psychologists, psychiatrists, and experts in the field. Until recently the advice about victims was that abuse did no long term harm and about child abusers was that their actions could be stopped and they could be cured. The priest was often sent away for treatment. Usually the doctors advised the bishops to put these men back into new assignments after getting from them a promise not to do this thing again. The priest was given a new assignment. There he began to abuse children once again.

When the history comes to light that there were complaints or rumors of abuse by the priest, and the bishop at that time knew this but gave the abuser a new assignment, the present victims are outraged. Often they are the ones who were abused in these subsequent assignments. We know now that the professional advice to put the abuser back into an assignment was incredibly bad advice, but that is the advantage of 20/20 hindsight.

When the issue of clergy abuse of children began to become news in the early 1980s the Catholic Church made some monumental mistakes in how it dealt with the issue. There were cases in Louisiana and other states where the bishops had absolutely no idea what to do, so the cases were turned over to lawyers who treated the victims with a harshness and cruelty that was truly unchristian.

Internally the American bishops had a hard time trying to decide what to do about the growing sexual abuse scandals. They enlisted the help of more psychologists, psychiatrists, and experts in the field who told them that all the old advice about putting abusers back to work was wrong. They now said that abusers could never be cured and could never go back into ministry.

The bishops came to an agreement about a three part plan. The first was to redo all the psychological testing and seminary evaluations processes so that pedophiles and potential abusers could be discovered before they became priests. The second was to ask the pope to rewrite church law so that bishops would have more authority to remove priests from ministry.

The third part of the plan was to approach those who have been victims of clergy abuse with much more care and concern and minister to them rather than just send lawyers after them.

Seminaries today use every possible means to discover applicants with any sexual dysfunctions. In the past ten years every diocese in America had developed a sexual abuse policy and every priest, sister, and all other employees have been mandated to attend ongoing workshops on sexual abuse.

It is hoped that the future will not bring to light cases of abuse by priests taking place today. But there are no guarantees.

That a priest could sexually abuse a child is still incomprehensible to me. I know the facts. It is a fact that the percentage of sexual abusers among the Catholic priesthood is no different from any other profession – teachers, policemen, businessmen, Protestant ministers, or any other. It is a fact that it is a serious mental illness, not just a weakness of the will. But it is also a fact that abuse is a serious sin, and one with enormous consequences for the victims, for all other priests, and for all the members of the Church and society. I believe that a priest who has abused a child should never be allowed to function as a priest again.

The abuse scandals have changed the lives of each victim, but they have also changed the lives of every priest. Thirty years ago priests were automatically totally trusted by parents and children – that is no longer true. One of the major causes of the clergy shortage is that parents often actively discourage their sons from even considering the priesthood because of the clergy abuse scandals.

I know some of the priests who have abused children and are now either in prison or who have left the priesthood. I know I am angry at what they have done, yet I also feel sorry for them. Sexual abuse devastates everyone it touches, victims, perpetrators, families, and all the rest of us as well.

She Was A Most Interesting Lady

I got word the other day that Spice Robertson died. While that is not her real name, it is close enough.

I met Spice one day years ago when she knocked on the door of my rural Idaho rectory. She had recently moved to town and wanted to meet the priest, to "check him out" she said so she could decide if she wanted to go to Mass here or travel somewhere else each Sunday. I guess I passed the test because Spice became part of the parish and part of my life.

Spice was a professional diner waitress – hard shell, gentle soul – right out of central casting. It took a long time until I really knew her story, her journey. Little Spice's parents were servants in the home of a wealthy couple. The couple insisted that she attend the local parochial school, the same the couple's own children had attended some years before. When eighth grade graduation came, the couple suggested that she attend a famous Catholic boarding school. This would mean leaving her school friends, but the advantages of a boarding school education for a girl in the late 1950's were too great to turn down.

Spice loved the school and while still shy and timid, excelled in everything. She also began to think about becoming a sister herself. When she finally mentioned this there was immediate acceptance of the idea both from her family and from the sisters. She graduated from high school in early May and was scheduled to enter the convent on August 15th.

Back home for the summer, Spice met up with some of her old friends. One of them invited her to a party at the house of someone from another school, someone Spice had never heard of. She thought about it and because she trusted her friend, she accepted.

Her friend told the guy hosting the party that she was bringing someone about to become a nun. He and his buddies thought it would be fun to get her drunk, and they did. She didn't know they had

137

spiked her drink. Then the guys took her upstairs and raped her. She tried to stop them but they were much too strong.

She was too embarrassed to tell anyone. In late July she realized that she was pregnant. Frightened and scared she left a note for her parents, wrote a letter to the sisters, and ran away from home to Chicago. She didn't tell anyone she was pregnant she just said she changed her mind about becoming a nun.

She gave birth to a son in a shelter in Chicago. She started her waitress career at an all night diner. Spice was convinced that she had sinned, that God and her parents would never again love her, and that she was a totally worthless human being.

Over the next twenty years she lived with a variety of men, always seeking someone to be a good father to her growing band of children, but usually finding someone who beat and abused her. Slowly she got involved in drinking, drugs, and even some prostitution.

Religion, church and God had all become just faint memories until a chance remark in a bar in Milwaukee. Someone saw the cross around her neck and challenged her that her language, her attitude, her life was such a contradiction to the cross she had no right to wear it. The cross was the one the sisters had given her for high school graduation, it was the only piece of her early life she had saved.

There was no quick overnight miraculous change for Spice, but gradually she began to think that maybe there was some hope for her after all. She met a good priest who helped get her back on the right path with God, and then she met a good man, Paul, a truck driver from Idaho who was the cause of her move west.

She had six children by six different men. The older two were sent to prison, but both have turned their lives around and are doing well now. The next two ended up in the sex industry. The fifth was in a drug rehabilitation program. The youngest, raised by a sober and good Spice, was a kind and sweet little girl.

I liked Spice, I liked her a lot. By the time I met her she had truly gotten her life together and was good friends with God. She had a lot to teach me.

With her permission I used to use her story in my teaching, especially about the consequences of sin. I would tell her story and then ask some questions:

The boys who got her drunk and raped her, is her life their fault?

What responsibilities do they have for what happened to her? What responsibility does she have for what happened to her? Hers was a life of such sadness and sorrow – who made all of that happen? And the man in the bar with the courage to tell her about the cross – is he responsible for her coming back to God?

She was a good lady, may she be enjoying God in the resurrection she so richly deserves.

October 28, 2000

Thank God For The Dead People Who Are Active In Our Lives

Few issues emphasize the fundamental differences between the various types of twenty-first century Christianity than that of dead people. The Catholics and Orthodox believe that the dead are an active and essential part of the lives of the living. Fundamentalists and many other types of Protestants believe that the dead have no active role in the lives of the living. Some of the mainline Protestant churches are in between.

We Catholics do not usually use the phrase "dead people" in speaking about this reality, we use the word "saints", or sometimes "poor souls." But realistically what we are talking about are people who have lived and then died.

Those who believe that saints have no active role in the lives of the living see our relationship with God as an individual one. Each person is to accept Jesus as his or her personal savior. Each person stands before God individually. The most anyone else – living or dead – can do is be a good example and provide encouragement. Saints are such good examples and they give us models to imitate, but they are not personally involved with people today.

Catholics understand saints in a totally different light because they see our relationship with God in a totally different light. Catholics believe that by baptism we become part of the People of God. God relates with us not only as individuals but as a people, a community. We can literally share the grace of God with one another, influence the spiritual lives of one another, participate in the relationship each of us has with God. Our souls are intertwined and interdependent. We never stand before God individually.

Because our lives and souls are so involved with the lives and souls of other people, it makes little difference whether those other people are alive or dead. They can still actively influence us, pray with and for us, share God's grace with us, support and sustain us. When our parent, spouse, neighbor dies, that is not the end of their relationship with us or their involvement in our lives.

But we do not even have to have known that person who died while he or she was on earth. The saints are intimately involved in the lives of all who call upon them, from all times and places. They are especially involved with those people and in those places where they have been asked for special patronage. Saint Francis of Assisi has a special real involvement in the parish in Bend, Saint Edward does the same in Sisters, and Saint Charles looks down and protects the hospital.

Saint Thomas of Canterbury and Saint Faucher (there really is a Saint Faucher, a 12th century French monk) are overworked a bit trying to help me, just as the patron saints of other people intercede and share grace with them. The saints are alive and active in the our lives.

Whenever we Catholics have a celebration of a major change in the lives of people such as Baptism, Ordination, the Blessing of a Church, etc. we call on the saints to be with us. We want the whole Church – living and dead – to be involved. We do this by an ancient prayer called the Litany of the Saints. We use that litany at Easter when we reaffirm our Baptismal promises. We do this because without the help and influence of the saints we could never keep those promises.

Sometimes people will tell me they can see no reason for saints, they would rather go directly to God. I don't understand that. That to me is like saying that in my family I will speak and relate only to my mother and father and ignore my sisters and brothers. Of course we pray to God directly and relate to God and have a relationship with God, and a personal relationship with Jesus. But part of that prayer and part of that relationship are my brothers and sisters – the saints.

In the 2000 year history of the Church there have been times when the devotion and role of the saints has been very healthy, and times when it has gotten way out of kilter. The medieval preoccupation with relics has never appealed to me, especially when I heard stories of how seventeen of the twelve apostles were buried in Germany alone, or one church which displayed the head of John the Baptist as a child.

Even today there are Catholics who give undue emphasis to devotion and acknowledgment of the saints, usually the Virgin Mary. The official Church casts a very skeptical eye at many of the modern alleged apparitions of Mary. As one bishop supposedly said, "If she is only going to half of those places, I would love to be her travel agent."

For the most part most of us Catholics have a good and healthy understanding of and relationship with the saints, even being able to joke about them as the bishop's quote shows. For Catholics the pictures and statues are just family photos, no more, no less.

Each official (canonized) saint has his or her feastday. Some of these everyone celebrates such as Saint Patrick's Day (March 17th) or Saint Valentine's Day (February 14th). For some the celebrations are a bit smaller, such as Saint Winefride (November 6th) or Saint Edward the Martyr (March 18th).

But just in case anyone gets left out, and to honor all of those who do not get canonized, on November 1st we celebrate the Feast of All Saints. It is the night before this feast of All Saints or All Hallows which comes down to us by its Anglo-Saxon name of All Hallows Eve, or Halloween.

As we celebrate Halloween this week, think of the saints, especially your patron saints, and give thanks to God through them.

November 25, 2000

Where Do I Fit In The Wide Spectrum Of Christianity?

Imagine a vast field with all the Christian people of every kind and variety. Imagine further that they are grouped by their fundamental beliefs and understandings of God, of Jesus, of the Bible, of sacraments, of salvation, of sin, of Church. Traditionally this would have put Catholics and Orthodox over in one end and Protestants at the other, with a large gap in between. There would be just a few denominations like the Episcopalians somewhere in that vast open space, but it would be mostly very empty.

But in what is one of the most important shifts in religiosity since the Reformation itself, that division is no longer accurate. Catholics and Orthodox would still be at one side, but not as far into the end as before. More importantly, the other end would be filled with evangelical, conservative, fundamentalist Protestants, whose numbers would be growing minute by minute. But other Protestants, especially the mainline Protestants, would have moved into that once open gap, leaving a narrow space between themselves and the Catholics and a wide and getting wider gap between themselves and the fundamentalists.

The causes for this massive change in the Protestant world are many, including the Catholic Second Vatican Council and the rise of fundamentalism itself, which was founded as a rejection of mainline Protestantism. The effects of this change in Protestantism are also many, including Protestants from mainline denominations in the military who feel more at home at Catholic Mass than at fundamentalist bible service, and interdenominational ministerial organizations which have split into only fundamentalists in one group and all others including non-Christians in another (such as happened in Bend.)

It is one thing for denominations to go through this kind of grouping, but how about people themselves. What follows are some basic statements about God, life, Jesus, and other topics. One statement reflects a more Catholic point of view, the other a more fundamentalist Protestant point of view. At the end there will be a key to which answer is which.

Please circle the letter for each numbered statement which most reflects your beliefs. Do this quickly, almost as if by instinct.

1. A. The world is basically filled with sin and evil.
    B. There is much goodness in the world which hints at God's goodness.
2. A. The good person must be deeply involved in the problems of the world.
    B. The good person must avoid contamination by the corruption in the world.
3. A. God is almost totally removed from the sinfulness of the world.
    B. God reveals himself in and through the world.
4. A. The Bible must always be interpreted using the context in which it was written.
    B. The Bible must always be interpreted as the literal word of God.
5. A. It is dangerous for humans to be too concerned about worldly things like art and music.
    B. Through such things as art and music we learn about God.
6. A. Harmony and cooperation are more common than strife and disorder.
    B. Strife and disorder are more common than harmony and cooperation.
7. A. Everything Christians believe must be verified in the Bible.
    B. Not everything Christians believe has to be verified in the Bible.
8. A. Almost everyone will be in heaven.
    B. Only a limited number of true believers will be in heaven.
9. A. Women who have a husband who can support them should not work outside the home.
    B. Women who have a husband who can support them should work outside the home if she feels it is something she chooses to do.
10. A. Each of us has a personal responsibility for the social needs of our communities.
    B. We are each responsible for ourselves and our immediate family and should not take on responsibility for other people.
11. A. Grace comes only directly from God.
    B. We can receive God's grace through other people.

12. A. The truths God has given us always need to be developed and clarified as time and circumstances change.

B. The truths God has given us to believe need no development.

13. A. God is very interested in our sins.

B. God is not interested in our sins but in the forgiveness of our sins.

14. A. Human nature is basically good.

B. Human nature is basically fundamentally perverse and corrupt.

15. A. We always stand alone as an individual before God.

B. We never stand alone as an individual before God, but always as an individual person who is part of a community.

16. A. There is great value to structured, ritualized, memorized regular prayer.

B. Only true authentic spontaneous prayer from the heart is effective.

17. A. Most human activity is vain and foolish.

B. Human activity helps reveal God in the world.

18. A. Our faith is always tied to the faith of the Church of which we are part.

B. Our faith is always only our own personal individual faith.

19. A. Every person must acknowledge Jesus as personal savior to be saved.

B. People can be saved without knowing Jesus by name.

20. A. Those who have died can still influence our faith and spiritual lives.

B. The dead cannot influence our faith and spiritual lives.

There are no right or wrong answers. Response "A" to the odd numbered statements tends to be a more fundamentalist response, as is response "B" to the even numbered statements. Conversely, response "B" to the odd numbered statements is more Catholic, as is response "A" to the even numbered statements.

If your responses tend to out of kilter with what kind of Christian you thought you were, it might be a good time to do some serious studying.

December 30, 2000

Questions To Ask As One Year Ends And A New Year Begins

Discussing the fact that life is a journey during a recent lunch with two deeply perceptive ladies, one of them mentioned the growing popularity of the medieval labyrinth. The labyrinth is not a maze in which we get lost, it is a hidden path in which we get found, a place to go and just think, listen, meditate.

Not everyone can find a physical labyrinth to walk, but the need to do so can still be very real. What follows is a sort of "labyrinth for the spirit." It is a series of questions to enable each of us to do some serious thinking.

It is best used by taking some time alone or with at most one or two other people. Some people might just want to think about the questions, others may want to write the answers out, maybe comparing the answers year by year. It can be used by couples contemplating marriage. It is a very adult level of questioning but some teenagers would also be able to use it well (maybe even with their parents).

1. Do I like the person I have become?
Who am I? What are my talents, my weaknesses, my virtues, my vices? Do I like myself? Would I want my son or daughter to marry someone like me? How much do I really know about myself? How much do I let others know? Can I stand to spend time by myself, or do I have to have distractions?

2. What role do my relationships with other people play in my life?
Who do I have relationships with? What are those relationships like? In my relationships do I act like an adult, a child, a friend, a parent, an owner, a controller, a servant, a serf? Are my relationships healthy? Why do I choose the people I do? Do I live up to my

committed relationships? What do blood relationships mean to me? Do I have alienated relationships? What do I get from keeping the alienation alive?

3. Do I believe in God?

What is the God like in whom I believe? What are the gods like I do not believe in? Why do I think about God the way I do? Where did my vision of God come from? Have I ever had any sense of a relationship with God? Do I communicate with God? Do I pray? Does God respond? Do God and I owe each other anything?

4. What roles do sex and sexuality play in my life?

Am I comfortable with my sexuality? Do I have any idea what role my sexuality plays in my life and decision making? Am I comfortable with the decisions I have made about sexual activity? How much importance do I give to sex? Is my sex life in balance with the rest of my life?

5. What are my values?

What are my real major values? Do I believe in right and/or wrong? Do I believe in sin and/or goodness? What role does my view of God play in my selection of values? Do I have good values for the wrong reasons?

6. How do I play, relax, enjoy myself?

What does play mean to me? How would I describe myself in terms of joy? Do I distinguish between joy and pleasure? Do I play at other's expense? Am I obsessive about play? Is my play a form of escape?

7. What is the foundation of my day to day existence?

Where do I stand? From where do I get my security and stability – myself, my ability, my spouse, my role as parent or spouse, God, my family name, money, my religion, my sex life, sports, or anything else? Why is that my foundation? Is it a good foundation?

8. What role does money play in my life?

What does money mean to me, both positively and negatively? Do I envy those with more money? Do I pity those with less money? Do I give money away? Do I equate money and worth? What would

I do for money? Is the value of money for me in acquiring it, hoarding it, controlling it, or spending it?

9. What role does control play in my life?

Do I always need to be in control? Do I always need someone to control me?   What does the idea of personal choice mean to me? Am I obsessed by choice? What do I think of authority? How much of my life is determined by control and authority issues? Am I a professional victim? Do I manipulate?

10. What does the reality of my inevitable death mean to me?

Have I ever actually admitted to myself that I am going to die? What do I think will happen to me when I die? Where does my understanding of God fit into my death? If I knew that I was to die tomorrow, what would I do? Am I afraid of my own death? For what would I give my life? For whom would I die? What is death?

I do not know anyone who can answer all of these questions easily; they are intended to be very difficult. But taken together they do form a labyrinth of the spirit, and are a great way to end one year and begin another. Happy New Year!

January 28, 2001

An Open Letter To A Young Couple Planning Marriage

Dear "Brad and Amy,"

It was good to see you a few weeks ago. I appreciate the request to send you some information about marriage. My comments in this letter about marriage are what I normally discuss with a couple coming in to be married. It is important that any discussion about marriage be forthright and honest. That is what I try to be.

There are two things I want to stress at the start. The most important thing for both of you to do is communicate, actually talk with one another. There is nothing as important as communication.

Secondly, you both need to make a strong distinction between the marriage and the wedding. The marriage is much more important than the wedding. A wedding should be designed to manifest the type of marriage you intend to have.

Because of this you both need to communicate about what you want your marriage relationship to be. You two need to discuss, really talk about, what each of you intends to happen when you get married. Being married is totally different than living together, which is the reason that most marriages of people who live together end in divorce.

There are two types of married relationships you can choose. The first one you will have, the second one you can choose to have.

Because you are going to be legally married, then the first type of relationship will be a simple contract marriage. An American legal marriage means that you intend to be married to each other only as long as both of you wish this to be true. If either of you decides to end the contract, you are free to do that by getting a divorce. This is the most common type of marriage in the United States today. This is the type of marriage most people your age choose to have. It is easier, it gives more freedom, it does not involve God, and there is an automatic escape clause. Simple contract marriages almost always end in divorce because they are basically intended to end in divorce. For the people who enter into those marriages it is a temporary situation usually for two to ten years. There is no real marriage preparation needed for a simple contract marriage. All you have to do is plan a wedding and show up.

The second type of relationship is a <u>spiritually bonded marriage</u>. This second type is much deeper than a simple contract and is absolutely permanent. A spiritually bonded marriage is caused by God uniting the two individual people. Many elements go into a spiritually bonded marriage, and it requires much preparation. There are criteria which must be met, promises to be made, maturity to be proven, etc. Weddings done by a priest or recognized by our church have to be spiritually bonded marriages, and that is increasingly true in other churches.

You two have to decide if each of you and/or both of you together: 1) want a spiritually bonded marriage; 2) are capable of a spiritually bonded marriage; 3) or would be happier and less threatened with just a simple contract marriage.

You need to ask yourselves and each other if either of you thinks your marriage will be temporary, only lasting for a couple of years. You are both smart enough to know that the fact that you presently love each other is not enough to make you stay together forever. If either of you thinks that divorce is probable or even possible, then you should have a simple contract marriage.

If you two end up choosing a simple contract marriage all you need to do is find a judge and schedule the ceremony. That is a very easy thing to do.

Do not underestimate the value of a simple contract marriage. You enter into a relationship knowing it is temporary, intended to last only a few years. When it is over there is probably sadness, but also a realization that it was always known that this would happen. Then each of you enters into another simple contract marriage. There are many people who are satisfied with one contract marriage after another. I am sure you know some of them. That is a legitimate choice in our society today, and it might be all you are capable of or what one or both of you want. If so, then honestly communicate that to your partner.

If a simple contract is what you want, then don't have children.

It is not fair to them. Get a dog or cat instead.

If you are convinced and committed that no matter what happens you will continue to be married, that your love is from God, and all the other criteria can be met, then you are able to enter into a spiritually bonded marriage. You need to begin the necessary work.

What you each have to do is get yourself personally ready to receive God in a new and different way. It is going to school to learn how to be married. There are usually some psychological testing, communication skill classes, financial discussions, moral discussions, parenting discussions, spiritual discussions. There can be sessions on what spirituality means, what children mean, and how to pray together.

The normal time line for all this is at least four to six months of schooling and preparation. This official preparation is often supplemented by work done by the couple on their own.

The one real mistake you two could make is to think that a successful [i.e. personally and spiritually happy and enduring] marriage just happens. It does not.

If you want a spiritually bonded marriage, then you need to get started on your preparation. I will be glad to help if you would like. Peace, Fr. Tom Faucher.

February 24, 2001

When Was The Last Time You Saw An Albigensian?

There are many things organized religion does well – accepting diversity is not one of them. Organized religion has a difficult time making a distinction between diversity and indifference. By accepting diversity I mean the ability to live side by side with fundamentally different viewpoints or convictions without compromising one's own beliefs. Indifference is believing that all viewpoints or convictions are equally valid.

Organized religion by its very nature relies upon a conviction on the part of the members that the belief system and moral conclusions of the religion are correct. Logically this means that conflicting belief systems and moral conclusions are wrong. For example, I believe that the doctrinal and moral teachings of the Roman Catholic Church are correct. Therefore I also believe that doctrines of other churches which conflict with Catholic teachings are wrong.

But if I have friends who are Mormon or Jew or fundamentalist or Christian Science practitioner how do I "accept the diversity" of their beliefs without being "indifferent" to their beliefs? And if I have friends who believe in moral actions which conflict with the moral teachings of my church such as abortion, suicide, living together, homosexual activity, how do I "accept the diversity" of their actions without being "indifferent" to their actions?

The traditional answer in medieval Catholicism was to accept no diversity from the teachings of the church, because all the people who believed wrongly or acted wrongly were committing sin, and would lose their souls. Efforts to stamp out conflicting views finally lead to the creation of the Inquisition, primarily to confront the heresy of Albigensianism. All the Albigensians were rounded up and ordered to recant. Those who refused were burned at the stake.

Did it work? It worked very well — when was the last time you saw an Albigensian? But new heresies kept cropping up and slowly the realization began to grow in my church that there was something terribly wrong with killing people because of their religious or moral convictions.

But the Inquisition took new forms in the Protestant world of England in the persecution of Catholics and in America with the witch trials of early Massachusetts. The United States has continued to have a sordid history of racism, sexism, anti-Semitism, and other forms of discrimination.

The accepting diversity/indifference issue today is still very real. Little fundamentalist children tell their Catholic, Jewish, Mormon classmates that they are going to go to hell because they don't believe correctly. Gay bashing and anti-homosexual behavior is common, making heros out of music icons such as Eminem. Even some ministerial associations reject other ministers who have slightly different beliefs. Are these actions good or bad?

To understand more about how difficult it is to accept diversity but not be indifferent, let us examine organized religion's treatment of sex. My church teaches that the only divinely blessed sexual activity is genital intercourse between a man and woman married to each other. All other sexual activity or any other combination of people is not right. Thus pre-marital sex, oral sex, same gender sex – these we do not believe to be morally correct.

The problem for the Catholic Church (and many other churches) is that the larger society sees nothing wrong with some of these activities. Pre-marital sex and living together are totally socially acceptable. All forms of sexual activity are acceptable, with oral sex now taking place in elementary school. Many people view same gender sex as totally acceptable. [In regard to these last two, the hypocrisy of American society is shown by imagining what would have been the reaction to President Clinton if the oral sex had been given by a Mark Lowinsky rather than a Monica.]

How should churches act when they believe that these behaviors are destroying those individuals doing them and they also must not be allowed to influence young children? Can a church member who believes homosexuality is a sin tell a gay person that he is going to hell? Can he shout it on the street? When couples come in to be married who are living together do we just ignore that? By marrying such couples are we just indifferent to moral behavior? Do we encourage or discourage gay promiscuity by opposing recognition of gay unions in any form?

A similar set of questions could be raised on the subjects such as belief systems, understandings of the Bible, or many other issues? If a fundamentalist believes that I as a Catholic am going to hell, does he have a right (or even obligation) to tell me that? Does a 10 year old fundamentalist have a right to say that to a 10 year old Catholic, Jew, or Mormon? How can I believe that Catholicism is correct and not tell everyone else that they are wrong? When does accepting diversity become indifference?

We all need to do a great deal of thinking and praying about accepting diversity and indifference? Here are five questions. They could serve well at the dinner table or with a diverse group of friends.

1) Are all religious belief systems equally true and valid? If so, then how can they differ? If not, then isn't it the responsibility of those which are true and valid to eliminate those which are not?

2) Is any sexual activity, by any combination of persons, moral and good? What makes a sexual action moral or immoral? Is it the action or the people involved? Where does faithfulness and commitment fit into sexual morality?

3) Does the Inquisition still exist today? If so, what form does it take?

4) Is there any difference between sexual activity such as oral or anal sex if the genders are different or the same? What would make such actions moral or immoral? Should gay couples living together be treated differently from straight couples living together?

5) Which is the mark of real maturity for an individual and a religion – uncompromising conviction, accepting diversity, or indifference?

Abuse Has No Part In Marriage

They were both young, probably mid twenties, married for about two years when I moved into the parish. Bob and Mary had no children. I remember the first time I met him was during Holy Week when we read the entire story of the passion of Jesus Christ. On the way out of church Bob stopped me and asked how someone could be so cruel, so barbaric to Jesus as to scourge him at the pillar and crown him with thorns. Mary just stood there, smiling while we talked.

One day I heard Mary was in the hospital. Someone called and told me she was there but under her maiden name, and not listed as a Catholic. I went up to see her and she was almost terrified when I walked into the room, telling me I should not be there, that if Bob found out that I knew she was in the hospital then things would get even worse.

Officially she had fallen off the back porch. That was her story and she was sticking to it. But the injuries were gruesome. I spoke to a nurse I knew and she said it was very obviously serious physical abuse, but they couldn't prove it.

A month later Mary was in the hospital again. My nurse friend had finally convinced her that she needed to do something. Mary wanted to talk to me. The story was all too familiar and all too frightening.

She and Bob had met at a Catholic college, hundreds of miles from their homes. They started going together their sophomore year. They met at a church function. He was funny, sincere, loving and kind. There had been one time during their courtship when Bob slapped Mary, but he was so apologetic and sorry that she brushed it off.

It was just before the wedding when she finally met Bob's parents. Mary thought they were a little odd. The father was outgoing and pleasant, the mother seemed distant and afraid.

After the wedding things changed radically for Bob and Mary. He became jealous and demanding. He began to treat her like his father treated his mother. Bob started hitting Mary. He was always sorry, always promised to never do it again, but it always happened. It wasn't drinking or drugs that triggered the abuse, it was stress.

I asked her what finally made her realize that she needed to leave him. Mary told me that her mother-in-law had come to see her in the hospital. The mother-in-law was furious at her and demanded, "What did you do that forced my poor boy to hit you that hard? I learned a long time ago that when my husband hits me it was always something I did that caused it." Mary could see her future and she did not want it.

Mary told Bob she wanted a divorce. He was shocked, totally surprised, absolutely amazed. He had no idea why she wanted a divorce. He loved her, he worshiped her, she was the center of his life. He promised to never hit her again, and anyway, hitting her wasn't that big a deal. She knew he didn't mean it.

Bob came to me, telling me to talk some sense into her. When I told him I was one of the people who encouraged her to get a divorce, he became angry at me. His father called me, asking me how I could call myself a Catholic priest and encourage a woman to leave his wonderful, outstanding, truly great Christian son. He told me I was a disgrace to the priesthood. He was going to report me to the bishop and even to the pope.

Mary moved back to her hometown, divorced Bob, lived with her parents. She got some serious professional counseling. Her marriage to Bob was found to be not the spiritual bond the church intends marriage to be, and she was able to marry again in the church. Today she has a wonderful husband and two great little kids. She sends me a card each Christmas.

Bob stopped coming to church. He found another woman and married her. The physical abuse continued and escalated until he was arrested for assaulting his second wife. He finally received some counseling, but it didn't seem to work. Assaults happened twice more until he was finally sent to jail. After his third divorce he stopped getting married.

Bob grew up in a family with physical abuse. His father beat up his mother. That is what he saw, he was taught abuse was normal. He was taught wrong.

Physical abuse is never normal, it is never acceptable. Physical abuse, like all forms of abuse, destroys love and destroys people.

In the eyes of the Catholic church one of the major purposes of marriage is the joy, happiness, and good of both spouses. It is the responsibility of each to promote the good of the other. Physical abuse does the total opposite.

I personally have a very difficult time seeing how a marriage in which there is physical abuse can ever be a truly valid marriage. The very first time that the husband hits the wife (or vice versa, something which is becoming more common) she should pack up and walk out. God is not in that relationship, only serious mental illness and/or evil are. Without early and very major intervention and counseling, that marriage has no hope of being a union of joy, happiness and good for both spouses.

There are some people who claim the name Christian who say that the husband should always dominate the wife. Even when this is manifested in abuse, the wife should endure that because marriage is forever, and the husband is always right.

Such ideas are pure nonsense and certainly not Christian. No one has a right to abuse another person. And just because two people went through a marriage ceremony does not mean that a real marriage took place.

One rule which should be remembered in any relationship, before or after a marriage ceremony — the first time one partner hits the other, everything has changed, and it will never go back. If they are not married, they probably shouldn't be. If they are married, they probably shouldn't be. God is not in that kind of relationship.

Physical abusers can be some of the nicest people. They are also either very sick or very evil. I met Bob socially about the time of his third marriage – maybe eight years after his divorce from Mary. He was still most entertaining, pleasant, and delightful. On the surface I guess he always will be

April 28, 2001

It Is Time To Honor Two Extraordinary Women

This time of the year – the Easter Season and the month of May – is the time when the two most important women in Christianity get the attention they deserve. They knew each other, traveled in the same circles, loved the same people. History, piety, and tradition have treated them with incredible fickleness, elevating the reputation of one almost to unreality, bringing the other down almost to the gutter with falsehoods and lies. The two women are of course Mary of Nazareth, mother of Jesus, and Mary Magdalene.

It comes as a surprise to many Christians to learn that in the early church, Mary Magdalene was a much more popular and important figure than Mary of Nazareth. It also comes as a surprise to learn that Mary Magdalene was never a prostitute.

This Mary came from Magdala, a small town on the Sea of Galilee. She was obviously wealthy and independent. She is the only New Testament woman who has a name on her own, not some man's mother, sister, daughter, etc. She financed Jesus and the apostles, paying their way to travel around the countryside.

Jesus had "cast seven devils" from her, usually a phrase which means she suffered from some form of epilepsy, and she became his follower. She was present at the crucifixion and saw where he was buried.

Mary Magdalene became critically important when she was the first person to discover the resurrection and the first person to see the Risen Christ. She became the "Apostle of Truth" dispatched to tell the good news of the Resurrection to the apostles. It was unheard of that a woman would be entrusted with a message for men – but the Risen Christ did precisely that with Mary Magdalene.

The records of the early church clearly show Mary Magdalene as an equal of the male apostles, a participant in their councils, and a source of their collective wisdom. The earliest church had a gender equality not matched since that time, and the center of it was Mary of Magdala.

But as Christianity become more established and eventually more Roman, the roles open to women began to reflect Roman society. A powerful, pushy, independent woman became less appealing than a pious, obedient, faithful one. The splendor of Mary Magdalene began to fade as the splendor of Mary, mother of Jesus, began to grow.

As Christians began to be Roman and Greek householders, family people, and respected citizens, not just converted slaves, gladiators, and soldiers, the image of the Virgin Mary, mother of Jesus, was saying something to them. She gave them a model for their own homes, their own lives.

Very early, before the Church had even finished writing the New Testament, the theologians and thinkers (often called the Fathers of the Church) were trying to understand who Jesus really was, where he came from, and how he could be both God and human. This also placed an emphasis on Mary his mother, and it started to become clear how important her role actually was.

Mary, mother of Jesus, was seen as the fulfillment of Old and New Testament prophecies, leading to the revelation and realization of her Immaculate Conception, her perpetual virginity, her role as *theotokos* (Mother of God), and her assumption into heaven. By the fourth and fifth centuries she was the image of the perfect virgin, the perfect mother, and the perfect woman.

As he prepared for his sermon for the feast of the Holy Cross (September 14), in 591, at San Clemente in Rome the very perfection of the Virgin Mary, mother of Jesus, was a problem for Pope Gregory the Great. He was beset with the difficulty of a number of women who had fallen away from the church and entered into lives of decadence and sin. Now they wanted to return but some within the church said they could not be forgiven.

The pope, long on compassion but short on knowledge of the Bible, combined the unnamed prostitute in the seventh chapter of Luke's Gospel with Mary the sister of Martha and Lazarus, and with Mary Magdalene. These three women became one person, a "Super Sinner," whom he named Mary Magdalene. His new Mary Magdalene was a prostitute who had been saved by the Lord and become the witness to the resurrection. If she could be forgiven, then anyone could be.

The pope's new sinner was an instant success. This new Mary Magdalene took off like hotcakes. A real honest to God sinful woman who had been forgiven and then became close to Jesus himself — she was one of the most popular subjects of sermons for the next thousand years.

The middle ages had Mary, mother of Jesus as the calm, holy, virginal, sinless, personification of human perfection, and Mary Magdalene as the sinful, lustful, prostitute whose life had been transformed by the Lord. Between them they covered all the bases.

When the Protestant Reformation tore medieval Europe apart, devotion and regard for saints went with the Catholics. Catholicism as a communal religion believed saints were fundamental to Christianity. Protestantism as an individualistic religion placed little or no value to saints. As Protestantism continued to splinter, some groups became increasingly opposed to saints, and especially to Mary, mother of Jesus. Protestant extremists even claimed that Catholics worshiped Mary. Only a few Protestant groups placed a high value to Mary, mother of Jesus, although some of them did name halfway houses for ex-prostitutes after Mary Magdalene.

As the twenty first century begins, scholars have discovered the tragic error of Pope Gregory and are beginning to restore Mary Magdalene to her rightful place as the Apostle of Truth and the most influential woman of the New Testament. Catholic Marian extremists have been curbed by Pope John Paul II and Vatican II, ensuring a good solid understanding of the Virgin Mary, mother of Jesus, in the Catholic church. Protestant church men and women have begun to reevaluate the role of Mary, mother of Jesus, in Protestant theology and devotion.

In the Lectionary, the book of readings used in many Christian denominations, the Easter Season is the time of Mary Magdalene. May is the traditional month to honor Mary, the mother of Jesus. Thanks to both for all they did and continue to do.

About the Author

A native Idahoan, Father Thomas Faucher was born and raised in Boise. He attended high school and the first two years of college at Mount Angel, Oregon. After graduation with a philosophy degree from Saint Thomas Seminary in Seattle, he received his next two degrees in systematic theology from Catholic University in Washington DC, with additional concentration in liturgy. He has also gained a degree in Canon Law and special training in sociology, church leadership and organizational management.

Ordained a Catholic priest in 1971, he has served in parish ministry in Rupert, American Falls, Pocatello, Emmett, McCall, and Boise in Idaho, as well as parishes in Maryland, Washington DC, and the Diocese of Wrexham in North Wales. He has served as Diocesan Director of Liturgy in both the Diocese of Boise and the Diocese of Baker, as Chairperson of the Federation of Diocesan Liturgical Commissions for the United States, as a member of the Advisory Board of the Bishops' Committee on the Liturgy, and as a member of the National Advisory Council of the National Conference of Catholic Bishops.

He has taught and lectured at Bishop Kelly High School in Boise, Idaho State University, Mount Angel Seminary, Saint Mary's College in Indiana, St. John's University in Minnesota, Hawkstone Hall in England, and Central Oregon Community College. His published writings include extensive columns and essays, two books, and contributions in theological and liturgical anthologies.

In 1996 he came to Central Oregon as Judicial Vicar of the Diocese of Baker and pastor of the Church of Saint Edward the Martyr in Sisters. His monthly column in *The Bulletin* newspaper in Bend, Oregon began in October of that year.